WAREHAM'S BASIC BUSINESS TYPES

BOOKS BY JOHN WAREHAM

WAREHAM'S BASIC BUSINESS TYPES

*Sorting Winners from Losers,
and Managing People for Profit*

JOHN WAREHAM

New York ATHENEUM *1987*

Library of Congress Cataloging-in-Publication Data

Wareham, John.
    Wareham's basic business types.

    1. Executives—Psychology. 2. Personality assessment.
3. Executives—Selection and appointment. 4. Success.
I. Title.
HD38.2.W37   1987   658.4'09   86-47686
ISBN 0-689-11756-6

I have been a student of human nature for a long time. I have associated, too, with many and diverse natures; and having observed side by side, with great closeness, both the good and the worthless among men, I conceived that I ought to write a book about the practices in life of either sort.

THEOPHRASTUS, *Characters*

ACKNOWLEDGMENTS

I'd like to acknowledge the help of my late chairman and colleague, the renowned psychologist Dr. Robert N. McMurry, who first seriously drew my attention to the concept of types: my editor, Ken Bowden, a closet psychologist himself, who suggested many first-rate additions and changes, and offered all kinds of wonderful encouragement; Anna-Louise Mole, for helping with all the corrections and offering useful and practical suggestions on the material; all the other fine people at Wareham Associates whose hard work permitted me the time and luxury of putting my thoughts to paper; and, of course, my wife, Margaret, who helped in more ways than could ever be adequately recorded.

CONTENTS

CONTENTS

CONTENTS

WAREHAM'S
BASIC
BUSINESS
TYPES

PROLOGUE
Overture, Warning, and Halfhearted Apologia

To foresee is to rule.
BLAISE PASCAL

A CLEAR UNDERSTANDING of personality types could make you a small fortune.

I speak from personal experience, for the best part of my life has been devoted to helping my clients sort winners from losers, and manage people for profit.

I began my own executive search and appraisal company a short generation ago. I recruited some wonderful people and we built a fine international firm, spanning three continents, so we must be doing something right.

That something is predicting human behavior with what can often seem to be astonishing accuracy. This is not a simple matter, for, as the old Chinese proverb has it, "Making prophecy is very difficult, especially regarding the future."

One of the important things I have learned is that the world—and especially the business world—is populated with

3

winners and losers, and that the key to picking winners entails knowing, in advance, as precisely as possible why some people will fail, whereas others will succeed. When you know the *why* of success or failure, you can sort people into clear types that allow you to make accurate professional assessments over and over and over again. If you don't know the *why* of human failure and success, then, however smart you may be, you're just guessing, and one day you'll guess wrong.

Consider for example:

Obviously impressed by John De Lorean's handsome face, charming manners, and supposed shining track record, the British government mistook him for an honest-to-God entrepreneur, thereby setting themselves up for the loss of more than $100 million dollars. This tragedy might have been avoided if only those in charge had known that Mr. De Lorean was not an executive at all, but just a highly dangerous "Gonnabee" (see page 76).

A large U.S. corporation hired a famous female M.B.A. whom the press had dubbed a "financial whiz." In fact, the "whiz" turned out to be both hopeless at figures and a witch to work with. She had to be "squeezed out," at great cost in dollars, heartache, and publicity—and none of it might have happened if the hiring chairman had known all about not-so-super "Supergirl" (see page 163).

A privately held company promoted its sales star to management ranks, only to see the pressure of the new role turn him into a raging alcoholic. It was a foreseeable—and avoidable—ending, if only the personnel director had known about the terrible "Tood" (see page 96).

Far from being rare or particularly notable, such tragedies represent the mere tip of a hiring-and-promotion iceberg carefully and deeply hidden from public gaze. The harsh truth, however, is that such errors are commonplace in nearly every organization in the land.

The paradox is that great amounts of time, thought, and heartache often precede these ghastly mistakes. A person is interviewed, checked out, tested and retested, prior to being wined, dined, wooed, and wed. Then, after failing on the job, he or she is eventually painfully dumped, with nobody quite knowing what went wrong. The standard cop-out, usually offered with a lame smile, is: "The chemistry wasn't right."

The *truth* is that somebody goofed. Somebody misjudged the candidate. Somebody failed to see the forest for the trees, because that somebody *failed to identify the basic personality type.*

And that somebody's failure is almost certain to have stemmed from one or more of the five basic fallacies of management evaluation. Let's quickly look at each of them:

The First Fallacy: "I can tell a lot by talking to someone."

An old saying has it that "every man complains of his memory, but no man complains of his judgment." This is nowhere more true than in a job interview, where even the most sophisticated and successful executives tend vastly to overrate their ability to reach valid conclusions after interrogating job candidates.

The simple fact is that, when it comes to conducting evaluatory interviews, most managers simply do not know what qualities they are looking for, and, in consequence, seldom have any clear idea of what questions they should be asking. Therefore, even if they should happen to ask a pertinent question, they rarely know how to interpret properly the candidate's answer.

The Second Fallacy: "Successful people go on being successful."

While this sounds like good common sense, it is actually the very nub of the Peter Principle, which, you will remember, argues that managers inevitably rise to their ordained levels of incompetence. In fact, most of those who do rise to such levels have been routinely elevated purely on the basis of their past successes. What is overlooked is that such successes are often *totally irrelevant to the tasks and challenges imposed by the promotion.*

The vital point to note, and never to forget, is that a record of prior success may have already brought the candidate to his or her "incompetence threshold"—the point beyond which he or she will *inevitably fail if further promoted.*

The Third Fallacy: "We minimize personnel mistakes by having several of our key people screen each candidate."

It is frequently believed that errors in hiring or promoting may be minimized by subjecting candidates to interviews by many people, or even to group interviews, so that a "consensus" can be reached. The rationale is that if two heads are better than one, then many heads should result in ultimate wisdom.

Any value in this approach depends upon the qualifications of the members of the committee. Mere size means nothing, for, as Émile Zola once crisply noted, "Even if fifty million Frenchmen say a foolish thing, it is still a foolish thing."

Unless at least one of the interviewers is blessed with special insight, then the whole exercise is a case of the blind leading the blind. Indeed, experience reveals that the combined judgment of lay interviewers is often *worse* than the individual opinions of the respective members.

6

A further point to note here is that group interviews—
"beauty contests," as they are sometimes called—heavily favor extroverted candidates, who tend to be highly adept in
such encounters, winning approbation for imagined personality strengths while actually diverting attention from indices
of personality weakness.

Thus, all too often, the job goes to the most charming,
physically attractive, or smooth-talking candidate.

The Fourth Fallacy: "References can be trusted."

References are suspect for several reasons. Most obviously,
references proffered by candidates are always likely to be
biased in their favor, and thus can seldom be taken at face
value.

Obtaining accurate references from past employers has become increasingly difficult, because fewer past employers are
willing to disclose adverse information about prior employees.
This is particularly true in cases where an employer fears that
a former employee might sue upon discovering that a bad—
albeit accurate—reference has been given to a prospective
new employer.

It must also be remembered that, even with the best will in
the world, *most referees are inadequately qualified to form an opinion as to the likelihood of a candidate's success in a new and more
demanding role.*

A referee may be trusted to verify the bare facts of a candidate's past employment. Beyond that, however, most opinions usually need to be discounted.

*The Fifth Fallacy: "Psychological testing enables us to resolve
tricky questions of hiring and promotion."*

Psychological testing has a part to play in management evaluation, but it has failed to provide the panacea promised in its
1950s heyday.

The problem with most popular forms of psychological
testing presently available to industry is not merely that the
results are highly unreliable, but that sophisticated test-takers
become adept at faking "correct" answers, thus attaining so-
called "executive profiles." In consequence, such tests tend to
be remarkably poor predictors of genuine business capability.

Are *any* tests reliable? Yes. Experts agree that "projective
tests" (like the famed Rorschach Inkblot Test, or the Ware-
ham/McMurry Incomplete Sentence Blank), calling for the
candidate to reveal his or her personality by psychological
projection, can be invaluable when properly administered and
analyzed by a qualified practitioner. However, these tests do
call for skilled interpretation, so they have not as yet enjoyed
wide use in industry.

It is also well to note that some personnel psychologists are
more skilled interpreters than others, just as in medicine some
doctors are better diagnosticians than others.

In all, psychological testing has been an art, not a science,
and therefore should be regarded at best as one tool, not *the*
tool, in the evaluation process.

The Real Key to Picking Winners

Consider the case of the large airline for which my New
York office was conducting a search to find a chief executive
officer. In the middle of the exercise, the chairman of the airline's board asked me also to appraise a fellow who was being

8

considered for the role of the company's legal counsel. After careful evaluation of the legal counsel, I personally called the chairman.

"Forget the CEO search, and hire this man for that job," I told him. The chairman and board members were nonplussed. "But he's just a lawyer," they argued.

"No, no, *no*," I replied. "He's *qualified* as a lawyer, but he has the *temperament* of a really great executive."

After a lot of toing and froing, for they'd been burned in the past, the board went along with my advice. Under the new man's leadership, the formerly ailing airline quickly took off, effecting one of the more spectacular turnarounds the industry has seen.

When it was all over, I had occasion to talk with the board members again, and, as you might guess, they wanted to know what it was in the new chief that had caught my eye.

The answer—so deceptively simple that they didn't believe me and put my judgment down to sheer luck—was that I'd collected enough data to know the fellow's *type*. I could see that the so-called lawyer was in fact one part "Emperor" and two parts "McCoy" (see pages 19 and 237)

The Secret of How the Basic Types Were Compiled

I'd like to take just a moment to share with you the secret of how I discovered my Basic Business Types, for I want you to understand that although the text might seem at times like a "fast read," the advice it offers is soundly and scientifically based.

In my firm, we approach the task of appraising people with considerable diligence. A lot of money—not to mention a person's life—rests on each of our analyses, so it is a job that just has to be done right for both business and moral reasons.*

First, we conduct a lengthy interview to elicit each candidate's entire life history. Next, we administer the psychological tests (both objective and projective) that we have painstakingly developed and validated over many years. After that, we run reference checks, and, if necessary, conduct further interviews. And it doesn't end there, either.

Always anxious to improve our methods, we track the future careers of the candidates whom we appraise. Then, finally, we commit both the data and our findings to a now quite massive computer data base.

It was in assembling this material that I discovered that people could be grouped according to type. I found, too, that, once I knew a person's basic type, I could foretell his or her future with quite astonishing accuracy.

Next, I found that knowing a person's basic type was something like getting hold of the overlay to a jigsaw puzzle. Without the overlay, nothing makes too much sense until all the pieces are fitted together. With the overlay, every piece makes perfect sense, so that assembling the puzzle becomes no challenge at all.

In the same way, once you know a person's type, you can make a highly accurate appraisal—*even from incomplete data.*

The Hidden Key to the Art of Expert Personality Appraisal

The key difference between expert and armchair psychologists is that the expert not only draws upon superior training

---

*Let's not be holier-than-thou, either: decent ethical standards make damned good business sense.

and experience, but also constantly accesses the bank of pre-vious cases he carries in his head, his *vocabulary of types*. Thus, the expert might be likened to a chess master who has mem-orized all the popular chess openings, and thereby outmaneu-vers his less skilled opponents through the simple expedient of placing his pieces in accordance with known success pat-terns.

Similarly, when called upon to appraise an executive for hiring or promotion, the expert psychologist automatically scans his mental files, comparing the new candidate with those analyzed in the past. If the expert has become thor-oughly familiar with such a type before, he is able quickly to render an accurate analysis of the new candidate. If the expert has *not* seen such a person before, he knows he is dealing with a new and possibly unusual situation that calls for special study and attention.

In a similar but even more sophisticated manner, I help my clients to slash errors of hiring and promotion by working from an increasingly sophisticated *electronic library of types*.

Nowadays, when called upon to appraise an executive, I collect and enter *all* relevant data—life history, psychological testing, reference checks, and interview impressions—into the computer, then compare the resulting pattern with the myriad of others already in the data base, thereby either determining the candidate's type or defining a whole new type.

Many people don't like being "pigeonholed," of course, claiming that we humans are far too complex to categorize. They also argue that reducing people to types is demeaning, and point to the words of Simone Weil: "Every being cries out silently to be read differently."

Like it or not, however, *Homo sapiens* can be typed, and typed very, very accurately, too. In fact, psychologists now agree that scientific "typing" can be the key to appraising anyone—executive colleague, friend, lover, spouse, even children.

In passing, I should say that some critics like to disapprove of Dr. Freud, and to proclaim that they "don't believe" in his work. In spite of this, I have presented many of my characters from a Freudian perspective, for barely a day goes by that I do not continue to be astonished by the accuracy of Freudian insight as it applies to the contemporary real-life cases I see. Were he alive today, I'm sure the good doctor would want to touch up his ideas and his terminology, and maybe even discard a theory or two, or part thereof. For the most part, however, if you ask me, he was pretty well right on the money.

How Best to Use This Book

This book of types was originally compiled for my own colleagues and clients. Hearing of the material, my publisher pressed me to allow the types to be brought before a wider audience. Now, as that happens, I feel a little like the French philosopher La Bruyère, who wrote, "The subject matter of this work being borrowed from the public, I now give back to it what it lent me."

You will find here an easy-to-read overview of some twenty-one types, together with handy checklists on each. There's also a listing of the real-life role models whom each particular type often likes to identify with, or to emulate.* Finally, each chapter contains hints on how to manage the type

---

*I might say that I know no more about these real-life personalities (all of whom seem to me to be fine, wonderful people) than is available in the media, and so nothing is intended to be read into their particular personalities by virtue of their inclusion in these pages.

under consideration, first to help you reduce errors of hiring and promotion, and then to go on to bring out the very best in those who do join your team.

You will also be able profitably to use much of the material in this book in your everyday nonbusiness life. Indeed, if you are presently contemplating taking a spouse, you may want to study some of these chapters *very* closely, for by so doing you could save yourself a lifetime in hell, or a fortune in legal fees, or both. You may or may not want to apply the collected wisdom contained herein to your friends. You will, however, always want to apply the material to acquaintances and colleagues seeking to tap you for loans, for such people inevitably become the firmest of enemies.

At this point, however, a caveat seems to be in order. Since this book *is* written to be *read*, and since people's little foibles can be very amusing, I fear—and I mean to say this with some little modesty—that you may choose merely to be entertained, without fully appreciating the profundity of the information and insights being made available to you. Accordingly, I must ask you not to be taken in by the colloquial and sometimes even ironic tone. Bear in mind that these are not mere caricatures, but real flesh-and-blood people. These are not only your employees, but virtually everyone you know. If you doubt me, think on the matter a little harder when you've finished the book.

The list of types is not exhaustive, of course. All of the people in business cannot be reduced to a mere twenty or so types. Just the same, if you read carefully and study closely, you might be just as surprised as I was when I first came to the profession of appraising executives, and was astonished to discover the universality of some basic business types. I was also amazed at the way in which people stay in the character of the type: Wooers really do woo, Gonnabees always are climbing, Boyscouts do follow orders, and McCoys really do perform.

There's a little of each of us in nearly every type, of course, which might complicate things if you want to determine *your* type. Armed with this book, however, you'll be in a position to do as I do and describe a person as, say, two parts Boyscout and one part Tapdancer. And, in the case of a person who seems not to clearly fit any type, you may want to follow my example and study that person very closely indeed, to the point if need be of building an entirely new profile.

If you're in business and playing for high stakes, and are in any doubt about how to handle a particular person, then by all means seek an objective outside professional evaluation.

Apology for the Author's Bad Taste

I'd also like to offer an early apology. Critiquing people runs counter to our culture. Not quite cricket, as the British like to say. In bad taste, even. Thus, some people are going to be offended by the fact that many of these characterizations are partly or wholly negative. My response is that I am guilty of telling the truth, which is that many apparently wonderful people can also be incompetent and foolish, vainglorious and vexing, vicious and vindictive—as a quick glance at your daily newspaper will confirm.

A Pollyanna approach on my part might please more people, and perhaps sell more copies of this book. Unfortunately, Pollyanna's sunny view of human nature would not be of much help to the practical business leader, for a person needs a calculating head in order to survive as a big fish in shark-and-piranha-infested water. Since I am paid to spare my clients from such animals, I am not always unhappy to expose the true colors of certain corporate climbers. Indeed, I tend to share Oscar Wilde's sentiment that, in such circumstances, "It becomes more than a moral duty to speak one's mind, it becomes a pleasure."

This also explains the preponderance of "losers" in these pages. My seeming fascination with failure stems from the fact that the key to predicting executive success lies, paradoxically, in looking very closely at any and all personality warts that might cause a person to fail, no matter how apparently trivial such blemishes may seem. For the higher a person climbs, the greater is the likelihood that he or she will be brought down by an Achilles' heel. A naive and carefree outlook would not unduly impair a spear-carrier, yet it could be the death of a warrior. Lear thus finally fell prey to his own naive views of human nature, Macbeth became the victim of his flawed integrity, and Hamlet failed on account of mere indecisiveness.

The bright side in all of this is that some people can change when the darker side of their own nature is held up to them. Not many, alas. But some.

The Types

If these characters are not liked, I shall be astonished;
and if they are, my astonishment will not be less.
JEAN DE LA BRUYÈRE, *The Characters*

I

In the only office boasting its own throne sits . . .

EMPEROR

*A man must have a certain sort of intelligence to make
a fortune, and above all a large fortune;
but it is neither a good nor fine, a grand nor a sublime,
a strong nor a delicate intellect.
I am at a loss to tell exactly what it is,
and shall be glad if someone would let me know.*
JEAN DE LA BRUYÈRE

AN EMPEROR is an outstanding business leader who
runs his business like a personal empire. An Emperor possesses the skill to achieve, the temperament to lead, and the
drive and creativity to grow. He also invariably possesses a
highly personal management style.

Lee Iacocca, Rupert Murdoch, and Estee Lauder are Emperors. So were Henry Ford, William Paley, and David Ogilvy.

Not all Emperors are as famous as these, however. Indeed,
most Emperors are more satisfied by achievement than by
fame, and would thus rather tend their fiefdoms than court a
high public profile.

Perhaps the most interesting thing about an Emperor is that
he is *not* a mysterious superperson, for his personality and
behavior normally conform to pretty clear patterns.

A unique sense of security and insecurity. Many people, perplexed by the Emperor's incredible drive, ask, "Is the Emperor well adjusted, or is he driven by some psychological demon, such as an inferiority complex?" The answer is "Both." The Emperor is well adjusted *and* insecure. He is well adjusted with regard to his own immediate family, yet he is insecure and driven to "prove himself" to the world at large. This combination is nicely illustrated in the roots of Lee Iacocca, who was raised to feel secure in his parents' love yet was mocked by childhood peers who sneered at his Italian roots.

Or, consider the case of the Australian-born media mega-magnate, Rupert Murdoch, who has inspired countless journalists to pose the question: "What makes Rupert run?" The answers lie in his upbringing, of course. Rupert Murdoch was raised by loving parents who primed him for success, giving him every opportunity to advance himself, including an Oxford education. However, young Rupert's colonial background and Aussie accent rendered him second-rate in the eyes of his priviliged Oxford peers, thereby perhaps provoking an underlying and ongoing sense of inferiority that drives him to prove his "specialness" to the world.

Although other elements come into the equation, this combination of security at home and insecurity in the world at large is so pivotal to the psyche of the Emperor that I'd like to explain it a little further.

A child denied real love or security at home grows up anxious. In adult life, he or she may suffer from both fear of failure *and* fear of success. Such feelings impair such a person's ability to function in any true executive role.

A genuinely secure childhood, on the other hand, produces

a guilt-free person capable of going out and just taking whatever he or she needs to attain psychic happiness. If life somehow puts such people in the position of having to justify themselves—to prove, by accomplishment, that they are not inferior—they are fully able to focus and harness all their strengths in order to make a grand showing, or "overcompensation."

The stuff of outstanding success is thus often ground into the child of loving immigrant parents, for the family nurtures a sense of security, yet the world provokes a sense of inferiority which the child feels bound somehow to overcome.

Is it possible, though, you might ask, for an Emperor to have been both insecure at home *and* insecure vis-à-vis the outside world? Might he not just be insecure, period? "Born having a breakdown," as was waggishly said of Yves St. Laurent? The answer is "Yes, but . . ."—and the but is that such a person usually falls victim to the self-sabotage syndrome, by somehow eventually torpedoing the very successes he seeks or attains. Such a person is not an Emperor but a Gonnabee, whom we'll look at more closely a little later.

High and often highly specific family expectations. An Emperor is normally raised in a home where business achievement is greatly prized. The Emperor's father, usually a successful businessman himself, instills profit awareness in his children. The Emperor grows up anticipating personal commercial success, just as some people from highly sports-oriented families expect to win in the athletic arena.

The Emperor also usually receives strong psychological reinforcement for following in the familial footsteps. Taught to prize accomplishment in a particular kind of business activity—be it real estate, publishing, cosmetics, whatever—that endeavor eventually literally becomes a *part* of him: it "gets in his blood." In Skinnerian terms, this means that involvement in the activity reinforces the activity, and that any success further compounds that reinforcement.

Thus, the Kennedy children are now reinforced by political activity, just as Lee Iacocca, whose father used to own a fleet of rental cars, is reinforced by the motor industry. Lee claims, of course, that he could have chosen any career, and he explains his "choice" by saying that he "just loves cars." The fact is that he just loves the memory of his dad, and being around cars rekindles good feelings in him about his father and his family.

Rupert Murdoch's father, a newspaper magnate, took great pains to try to ensure young Rupert's success in the media business. The story is told of how the old man pored over Rupert's letters from Oxford, hoping to discover a journalistic flair. Then, one day, reading just such a letter, he turned to his wife and happily cried, "He's got it! By George, I think he's got it!"

Some biographers have also said that a particular and continuing spur for Rupert Murdoch lies in the fact that he has yet to win the kind of unstinting esteem accorded to his knighted father, asserting that an unconscious wish to equal his father's standing is evident in Rupert Murdoch's widely quoted and very revealing remark that to accept a knighthood is to admit to "selling out."

Boundless energy and drive. Emperors are blessed with boundless energy that they just have to expend, and this is important for two reasons. First, achievement takes effort. Second, such a person is more likely to perform well under continuing pressure, for it will take that much more pressure seriously to upset him.

The important point, of course, is that the Emperor channels virtually all this superabundant energy into his work. He does this for two reasons. The first is to fulfill high familial expectations by becoming an outstanding achiever. The second is a response to a superego laden with work-ethic values. Thus, responding to unconscious demons, the Emperor is a person of obsessive drive, who just *has* to be working always.

Acumen. Everyone agrees that the Emperor is "smart," but what *is* smart? And how does one get smart? This intriguing question goes to the center of the Emperor's psyche.

I define acumen as a blend of knowledge, intellect, intuition, persuasive skills, and—most importantly—mature good judgment, the kind of judgment that enables a person to take the long view. A person possessing this kind of judgment realizes that short-term victories, however profitable they may seem, aren't worth much unless they also contribute to long-term goals.

The smart executive is thus also an honest executive, although not necessarily out of moral scruple. What often keeps the executive honest is the belief that underhand behavior is worse than immoral by being potentially injurious to his bottom line. Realizing that a reputation for integrity will better help him to gain his business goals, he cultivates an upstanding reputation by the simple expedient of *being* just as honest as he believes he has to be in his business dealings. He may be tough, mean, and ruthless, but he never makes the mistake of becoming a crook.

People can be smart yet dishonest, of course, as illustrated by the senior executives at E. F. Hutton, the large stockbroking concern that in 1985 admitted fraudulent and criminal dealings. Would the late E. F. Hutton himself ever have done such a thing? The answer is never in a million years! No man wise enough to create such an empire would be part of such a scheme. As a true Emperor, he would instinctively *know* that such dealings would constipate the goose that ought to be laying the golden egg. Mr. Hutton's successors, on the other hand, grew too clever or too greedy for their own good, and got the egg all over their faces.

From whence does our Emperor derive his special wisdom? The short answer is that he gets it from his parents.

Not every son of a wise man grows up smart, but a smart kid quickly learns from smart parents. Soon enough, he acquires smart cognitive processes, actually seeing the world through lenses ground by his parents, and learning to make acute judgments unimpaired by sentimental baggage. Or, to put it more simply, he acquires both common sense and the knack of applying it.

The wise parent also raises his progeny to become self-reliant at an early age, thus fostering survival skills along with what we call "street smarts." Being street-smart, after all, merely means being able to survive by one's wits in difficult circumstances.

A further point, too, is that the Emperor usually just *knows* more about his business than other people. And why not? In most cases, he is exposed to business early in life, and is overtly applauded and covertly rewarded for learning about it. Thus, the more knowledge he acquires, the more he wants to obtain. An example:

After acquiring a London newspaper, and wanting to convert the size from broadsheet to tabloid, Rupert Murdoch was told by his printers that this would be impossible, because the presses he had bought with the papers simply couldn't print the tabloid size. "We'll see about that," said Rupert, leading his printers into the bowels of the plant and trouping them to the special equipment needed to modify the presses. Murdoch wasn't using any special insight. He just *knew* from a quick glance at the machines that they had been made to be modified, and that the modifying equipment ought to be lying around somewhere.

An Emperor absorbs this kind of knowledge in the same way that some people easily remember baseball scores or other useless trivia. And the Emperor remembers it because he really *enjoys* knowing it.

Creativity and a philosophy. A bureaucrat follows orders and operates an existing structure, whereas an Emperor normally creates a new structure. Invariably it is a structure that is vastly superior to the old one, and much more conducive to the Emperor's ends.

Adman David Ogilvy, a Scot, devised a particular way of looking at advertising that enabled him to establish a highly successful business on Madison Avenue. Beginning with the premise that advertising should look like news, Ogilvy devised specific strategies for achieving that end, including fairly rigid policies with regard not only to the form of the idea, but also to the means of expressing it, from overall layout and illustration right on down to the size and style of type to be used.

From that point on, David Ogilvy wasn't so much an advertising man as the promoter of his own philosophy. He taught his disciples to think as he thought, and to create his kind of advertising campaigns, which they did with great success throughout the world.

Rupert Murdoch also assembled a philosophy, then turned it into a practical approach that enabled him to breathe new life into apparently unprofitable news media. His contribution to publishing might be summed up in a fairly simple notion: sell more papers by appealing to more people. His critics argue, often vehemently, that he achieves this goal chiefly by pitching his papers to people's baser instincts, by including in them such things as lottery games and frequent photos of naked ladies.

In fact, Murdoch's philosophy is much more sophisticated, and, like that of David Ogilvy, it also cleverly exploits such matters as page layout, column width, and typography. This, of course, doesn't solve the problem that many fainthearted journalists don't like to feel they are in the business of pandering to public taste, or going after the lowest common denominator, especially under the tutelage of an immigrant. In the end, however, the sheer success of the Murdoch philosophy, plus the gusto with which it has been promoted, has simply overwhelmed all opposition.

Many people, and not just reporters, feel demeaned by the idea of working to a formula. The fact is, however, that the majority of people have neither the intellect nor the emotional equipment to develop and work to a philosophy of their own creation. Accordingly, although they may protest otherwise, such people are secretly pleased and relieved to be shown or told how to earn a living, and the more specifically the better. Let's not be coy about it, either: a code that actually works, and which can be clearly taught and fully protected, is worth a fortune. Indeed, that's what the franchising industry is all about.

The Emperor's philosophy goes far beyond the merely technical aspects of the industry with which he is associated. Invariably, it will embrace codes of doing business with others, and frequently even *a way of living one's life*. Sometimes the credo will actually be spelled out, as used to be the case at IBM under Thomas Watson, where managers were obliged to assemble close-cropped, white-shirted, dark-suited employees for the singing of hymns and the like. Usually, however, the message is more subtly expressed, and simply filters down through the organization, gradually becoming a natural part

26

of the employees' lives, until eventually they become more than mere workers, absorbing the Emperor's entire outlook on life, adopting his mien and mannerisms, sometimes even his hue: indeed, becoming all in all his true disciples.

And, so long as the Emperor is a decent fellow, what could be nicer?

Persuasive and negotiating abilities. Emperors are invariably charming fellows. However, the charm is usually deceptive, masking the Emperor's steely and unrelenting determination to have his own way. Frequently, it also acts as lubricant for his penetrating negotiating skills, which are largely what get him his own way.

This is not to suggest that the Emperor is an oily fellow in the manner, say, of the archetypal used-car salesman. No, the Emperor's charm is much more regal, and therefore much more seductive.

You have to remember that an Emperor spends a great deal of his time putting together deals that will make his great empire even greater, so he has to possess both the ability to negotiate and the charm to consummate. Thus, if he did not already possess such skills, he would need to acquire them. And, invariably, he is blessed with the capacity to develop such powers, so much so, in fact, that you might be excused for inquiring as to the source of the savvy and charm that suffuse the Emperor's aura.

The answer, once again, lies in looking to the Emperor's parents. Such skills seem to derive from excellent negotiating ability on the part of at least one parent, coupled with an intensely loving relationship between at least one parent and the child.

If this intensely loving relationship was between father and son, then the son usually relates extremely well to every high-ranking businessman he ever meets. If that close attachment was between mother and son, however, then the son's charm is likely to be even greater, for he will almost certainly spend his life attempting to regain that motherly affection, while also harboring an unconscious and engaging desire to overcome or seduce virtually any prospect. Which is, of course, why he so loves making deals.

A female Emperor, on the other hand, is almost certain to have derived both her charm and her negotiating ability from her father, which, if you are still with me to this point, is probably what you were anticipating.

The Emperor's Management Style

The Emperor's management style is that of the benevolent autocrat, whose right to lead springs from his competence, his common sense, and his *joie de vivre*. He enjoys his work immensely, and he knows so much about it that he often cannot resist telling his subordinates how to perform their jobs even when they are almost as expert as he is. Indeed, he will even go to the shop floor or factory and *show* them how, and it is fairly common for legends to spring from this somewhat endearing characteristic.

The Emperor is normally too well adjusted to be imperious with his own people, whom he often regards with affection for being part of his "team," or, as he might sometimes even think of it, his "family." He detests incompetence, however, and thus may be ruthless in terminating people who display ongoing sloppiness or stupidity.

To sum him up, the Emperor is a true leader, whose power springs largely from his insatiable drive to achieve. His people stay motivated because the Emperor invests his work—and therefore their work—with a sense of special significance.

"*Nothing* is more important than the job we're doing," he tells his disciples, time and time and time again. He's not pretending, either, for the Emperor adores his work and *nothing ever* could be more important to *him.* Never knowing such a passion themselves, most people are thrilled to share his, and thus the Emperor carries them along, often changing their lives, and usually for the better.

When you get right down to it, the Emperor satisfies a basic human need: he authenticates our existence. He satisfies the desire to do something worthwhile—glorious, even—thereby enabling us to prove to ourselves (and to future generations, we hope) that we not only lived, but that we used our lives to change things for the better.

EMPEROR IN BRIEF

BASIC TYPE:	Founder and/or creative force behind a business empire.
ROLE MODELS/HEROES:	Own father. Lee Iacocca. William Paley. John D. Rockefeller.
FACADE:	Charming, no-nonsense, realistic, pragmatic.
COFFEE-TABLE LITERATURE:	*Harvard Business Review.*
FAVORITE SAYING:	"Let's *do* it."
APPARENT OBJECTIVE:	To lead a successful business empire to ever greater heights.
REAL OBJECTIVES:	To fulfill high familial expectations. To compensate for a sense of inferiority relative to forces outside his family.
UNDERLYING EMOTIONS:	Aggressive, steely, guilt-free, untroubled by self-doubt but still driven to "prove himself."
BEDSIDE READING:	*Iacocca,* by Lee Iacocca.
MIGHT BENEFIT FROM READING:	*The Rubaiyat of Omar Khayyam.* The Book of Ecclesiastes.

1. EMPEROR

MANAGEMENT STYLE:	Benevolent autocrat.
STRENGTHS:	Energy, acumen, creativity, negotiating ability, charm, strength under pressure.
WEAKNESS:	Not always understanding of insecurity in others, so can sometimes be a poor judge of people—thinks they are as well adjusted as he is. No major flaws, though.
HOW TO SPOT:	Father is or was a successful businessman, often highly so.

Extremely ambitious.

Usually eldest child.

Record of success in practically everything he touches.

Quick learner.

Many interests, and can turn his hand to virtually anything.

Strong technical industry understanding.

Usually shows a record of election to leadership roles.

Charming but not unctuous.

Possesses genuine presence or charisma.

2

At the top of the tree lives . . .

QUEEN BEE

Such women are men in skirts.
DR. ROBERT N. MCMURRY

THE QUEEN BEE is a force to be reckoned with, somebody special, an outstanding executive. Her exterior style is calm, charming, tactful. That's because she's a tough, smart operator: in fact, so tough and so smart that she never has to pretend to be either, and thus never has to raise her voice or draw blood to get what she wants.

The Queen Bee is also a source of endless wonderment to those who feel that women can't cut it in the boardroom with the big boys. "What makes her tick, what makes *her* special?" cry the chauvinists of both sexes.

Except for the fact that she just happens to be female, the Queen Bee's makeup is virtually indistinguishable from that of the Emperor. Like him, she is imbued with almost boundless energy, is a workaholic, gets along with pretty well everyone, and is blessed with first-class business judgment.

The Queen Bee, too, is the child of a happy home, where she was almost certainly raised by devoted upper-middle-class parents, who expected her to become an outstanding success. The key to her doing so is contained in her relationship with her father. She will have been his "special girl," the apple of his eye, the son he never had. The Queen Bee's father is likely to have been a successful businessman on his own terms, plus a well-balanced fellow who gave his daughter a lot of love, attention, and encouragement. He also instilled traditional male values in her, teaching her to prize tough-mindedness, achievement, hard work, the smarts, and success in open competition. Above all, he raised her to believe that she was "special," but without ever spoiling her.

The Queen Bee's motivation springs from a deep need to please her father, with the sexual element always present in such relationships sublimated in her pursuit and attainment of business success. Like the Emperor, the Queen Bee is also driven to show the world at large that she is a real honest-to-goodness achiever and an outstanding *person.* The Queen Bee never complains about being held back by virtue of her sex, but neither does she flaunt her sexuality.

If you spoke to a Queen Bee about any need to prove herself as good as a man, she would probably just laugh and tell you that she doesn't think that way. And, on one plane, she's telling the truth, for the issue is never of conscious concern to her, any more than humble origins—or whatever—seemed to bother the Emperor. On an unconscious plane, however, these underlying concerns are a wonderful source of irritation, to the point of constituting the dirt that makes the pearl, the manure that makes the rose, the sting that makes the Queen.

Idiosyncrasies of the Queen Bee

The Queen Bee likes the world much the way it is, thus is almost never an out-and-out placard-waving feminist. Quite apart from the fact that she's not by nature a complainer, she's

33

also very proud of having fully earned the right to the special treatment she receives. She knows she's a hard worker who has made sacrifices; she also feels that nobody has ever just given her something for nothing. Thus, she sees what is no more than the plain truth, which is that she really *is* a better person than practically all of the men and women whom she has outdistanced in business achievements, and probably in other fields also.

Though not at all haughty or affected, the Queen Bee can sometimes come off as unduly tough on wimps, naysayers, and also-rans: Margaret Thatcher thus scathingly refers to her own not-so-hard-nosed parliamentary colleagues as "wets." In this, the Queen Bee is no harsher than the Emperor, of course, but, irrespective of her position, people somehow expect a woman to be warmer and softer, more forgiving and nurturing, than a tough-minded male.

Mating Patterns of the Queen Bee

The Queen Bee commonly suffers considerable difficulty in finding a satisfactory long-term mate. This is understandable, for she is caught in a double bind. Her psychic imprinting calls for her to bed a hard-driving male like Daddy, yet very few males, even the truly confident ones, have been conditioned to seek such a tough and dynamic achiever for a wife. A purely physical factor comes into play, too, for, being a person of immense energy, and having been raised by a loving father, the Queen Bee is possessed of an intense libidinous drive that must somehow be sated, which can become a somewhat exhausting chore for any mate, following the fading of the first flush of passion.

The consequence of all this is that, where the Queen Bee cannot sublimate all of her drive into her work, she will often find herself engaged in carnal congress with the kind of man who *is* attracted to strong women. And, since such a man is usually some kind of wimp seeking a surrogate mother, the relationship is very rarely satisfying to the Queen Bee. Thus, she may well run through—or over—a series of submissive drones during her lifetime, perhaps marrying and divorcing several of them. Indeed, research shows that the typical top female executive is five times more likely to have been divorced than her male counterpart.

Like any achievement-oriented person, the Queen Bee is driven to excel in *all* areas of her life. Thus, when a union lasts long enough to be blessed with progeny, she may well set out to show, and succeed in showing, that she is just as great a mother as she is a business executive. Proud of this further achievement, the Queen Bee tends to be highly skeptical of any woman who complains of difficulty in running both a career and a family. "I do it, so why can't they?" she often says. What she usually fails to recognize or admit is that her resources are so much greater. She has more energy, is stronger emotionally, and, usually, she has more money, too.

Queen Bees and strident feminists can thus, paradoxically, wind up as adversaries, for the Queen Bee can appear to constitute *both* the embodiment of *and* a living contradiction to some fundamental tenets of the women's movement. The Queen Bee doesn't *play* at being an executive, she doesn't wear imitation male garb to the office, and she doesn't attend assertiveness-training seminars. She *is* accepted, however, totally and without question, in a "man's world," for she really is a big success. The reason is that she is an authentic person, a great executive, and a force to be reckoned with in her own right.

Or, as Don Corleone might have it, "a woman with balls."

QUEEN BEE IN BRIEF

BASIC TYPE:	Outstanding female executive or entrepreneur.
ROLE MODELS/HEROES:	Margaret Thatcher, British prime minister. Indira Gandhi, former Indian prime minister. Estee Lauder, cosmetics queen.
FACADE:	Charming, warm, confident, poised.
COFFEE-TABLE LITERATURE:	*Harvard Business Review. In Search of Excellence,* by Thomas J. Peters and Robert H. Waterman, Jr.
FAVORITE SAYINGS:	"My father always used to say anything's possible if you give it your best shot." "Frankly, I'm very glad to have been born a woman."
APPARENT OBJECTIVE:	To achieve, to be the best.
REAL OBJECTIVE:	To achieve, to be the best, thereby making good on the subconscious psychic understanding reached with her father.
UNDERLYING EMOTIONS:	Ambition, aggression, steely determination to dominate.

2. QUEEN BEE

BEDSIDE READING:	*Iacocca*, by Lee Iacocca. *Harvard Business Review.*
MIGHT BENEFIT FROM READING:	*Men and Women of the Corporation*, by Rosabeth Moss Kanter.
MANAGEMENT STYLE:	Benevolent autocrat.
STRENGTHS:	Energy, industry, judgment, cool head.
WEAKNESSES:	No major flaws. Minor flaw might be lack of a stable domestic support system.
HOW TO SPOT:	Only or eldest child. Outstanding history of achievement in most phases of life. Charming, but not overtly manipulative. Tactful. Often mentions father, clearly as role model. Feels confident in her success. Has almost always been in line management. First-class presentation. Discreetly well dressed. Does not wear imitation male uniform. Likely to have been divorced. Current husband or beau often

either passive drone, or altogether a totally well-adjusted person, happy to share in Queen Bee's success.

HOW TO MANAGE: Give her all the responsibility she can handle—then get out of her way.

3

Always within earshot of the chief...

SIDEKICK

*There is little serenity comparable to the serenity of the inexperienced
giving advice to the experienced.*
HENRY S. HASKINS

It's a true proverb that if you live with a lame man, you will learn to limp.
PLUTARCH

THE TWIN ROLES of chief and Sidekick are enshrined in literature: Don Quixote had his Sancho, Lear his Fool, Holmes his Watson, Batman his Robin, the Lone Ranger his Tonto. Politicians have Sidekicks, too: John Kennedy had his brother Bobby, Nixon had his Haldeman, Carter his Ham, Reagan his Laxalt. The English refer to Sidekick as a "PA," or personal assistant. Australians often call him "me mate."

Sidekick's major role is that of close associate and supporter, and in executing it he plays many parts and satisfies many needs, both spoken and unspoken. He is adviser, alter ego, priest, cheerleader, fortune-teller, gofer, hatchet-wielder, yes-man, whipping boy, and scapegoat.

Sidekick is much more than a secretary or an assistant, and often much more than a spouse. A spouse may sometimes

39

hold the job, but this is unusual, for Sidekick and chief usually share the same gender. There are good reasons why, the major one being that the relationship between the two can become hopelessly fouled whenever it becomes physical. And, of course, a large part of Sidekick's role is to anticipate and gratify the chief's ego needs in ways that a spouse, however loving, can rarely manage.

Close analysis of the Sidekick role reveals two types of Sidekick, the right-handed and the left-handed. A strong leader normally chooses a right-handed version, whereas a weak leader inevitably recruits the left-handed one.

Righthand—A Decent and Dexterous Administrator

Righthand is a strong, direct, capable administrator. Such a person is normally a crisp, capable, common-sense fellow, who does the job to the best of his abilities while endeavoring to serve the organization rather than just its chief—sometimes even to the point of making executive decisions in the chief's absence.

Righthand's major asset is his rationality. Righthand's clearheaded, logical approach both contrasts and complements an Emperor's infinitely more intuitive style. Where the Emperor is creative and often impulsive, Righthand is cool and analytical. A true executive, Righthand helps his Emperor to formalize ideas, and then goes on both to implement and to execute the resultant policies or decisions.

After watching Righthand in action, many observers confuse management skill with leadership ability, and feel that Righthand could found and direct his own enterprise. The truth is that although he is a great executive, Righthand's capacity to lead is fundamentally impaired by his own greatest strength: he is just too coolly rational to possess either the intuitive-creative assets or the warmth of personality that a truly great leader must own and use in order to found and maintain any great entrepreneurial enterprise. Thus, by virtue of authority conferred upon him, Righthand is good at issuing orders and *directing*. What he cannot do, however, is conjure the kind of empathetic understanding that is crucial to true leadership ability. Subordinates and colleagues just do not automatically pledge Righthand the same kind of allegiance that the Emperor, by virtue of his personal charisma, unstintingly commands.

Thus, in the course of his career, Righthand normally rises to the *role* of leader, but seldom makes a great fist of it, becoming, at best, a highly competent and highly paid professional administrator. A classic example of the role might be Frank Stanton, who played Righthand to Emperor Bill Paley in the halcyon days of CBS.

Lefthand—A Weak and Sinister Sidekick

Originally, the word *sinister* actually meant left-handed, and carried connotations of being elliptical, devious, or underhand. Thus, even today, we can properly define the left-handed Sidekick as an innately weak and passive but Machiavellian-minded wimp, who seeks and enjoys the kind of secondhand influence and status that can be parlayed from *proximity* to real power and true celebrity.

Lefthand craves this kind of essentially hollow gratification precisely because he *is* weak, as a means of easing his deep-seated feelings of worthlessness and helplessness, which prevent him from ever winning genuine power in open competition, or even, indeed—for fear of rejection—from simply throwing his hat into the arena. Thus, to obtain power he must *usurp* it, but, before he can do that, he must first get close to it. The Sidekick role thus holds enormous appeal for Lefthand.

As adviser to a great man, Lefthand will enjoy a kind of collective machismo, seeming to the world at large to be as strong as his chief. He will also have status without responsibility, for if anything goes wrong, the chief will be blamed, never his Sidekick.

Lefthand's innate weaknesses will not, of course, be tempered by his elevation to the role. Proximity to power will, however, almost certainly render him more superficially attractive to others. Even if Lefthand has little or no influence over the chief, other people will usually believe that he has, and this perception invariably invests him with a kind of pseudo power. People who normally wouldn't give Lefthand the time of day suddenly hanker to be his friend when they find that he has the ear of the Emperor. They toady to Lefthand, laugh at his jokes, share their intimacies, solicit his opinions, listen carefully to his (always guarded) replies, and then later wonder at his well-honed talent for obfuscation.

Lefthand usually doesn't have to do an awful lot in return for this unappetizing fawning. The unspoken understanding is that he will advance the supplicant's cause—or at least not torpedo it. Usually, all that is required is for Lefthand simply to choose a good moment to drop the supplicant's name into the Great One's consciousness. However, Lefthand exercises extreme caution even in doing so little as that, for, mindful of his own survival needs, he never wants to give the chief even the slightest sense of being pushed. Thus, all moves on Lefthand's part tend to be elliptical or Byzantine.

Nevertheless, this does not prevent the typical Lefthand from gaining far-reaching influence over his chief, as we shall see.

The Relationship Between Lefthand and His Chief

The relationship between chief and Lefthand is symbiotic, of course, for the parties are utterly dependent upon one another. Wimpish Lefthand can do little or nothing on his own, and thus needs a strong leader to manipulate. Lefthand also wants a chief-type figure to provide him with a sense of identity and purpose, and to protect him by helping conceal his weaknesses from both the world and himself.

What also needs to be comprehended is that the kind of chief prepared to fill Lefthand's vacuum does so in return for favors that are not entirely dissimilar. More than a few weaknesses thus lie hidden behind such a chief's own macho mask.

If asked to define Lefthand's role, this kind of chief will normally say that he is looking for a strong, ambitious subordinate capable of coming up with ideas of his own, and initiating independent action. What this chief *really* wants, however, is an emotional crutch to prop up his ego and keep his regal mask from slipping; to be able to "think out loud" before a silent but admiring sounding board, and to possess a cipher to implement—or ignore—the "ideas" so generated. Thus, initially anyway, Lefthand could, without too many people noticing, just as well be a cardboard figure.

In practice, Lefthand attracts the chief's eye, wins the job, and holds it largely as a result of well-honed groveling skills, along with a yes-man predisposition well and truly in tune with the chief's quickly evaluated neurotic ego-needs. A universal trait of all Lefthands is great deference. The chief is treated always with elaborate respect, to the point of actually being called "Chief." Most often, however, he receives his fuller title, which is "Yeschief."

Lefthand also usually assumes responsibility for getting

others both inside and outside the organization to kowtow to the chief. Lefthand sees to it that stories highly flattering to the chief are spread about, thus creating, it is hoped, a sense that the fellow might just be some kind of genius, or even a minor god. Of course, Lefthand also ensures that the chief knows the source of these tales, just as he also tries to give the impression that they are true—or if demonstrably false, at least that they *ought* to be true of such a marvelous personage.

As their relationship ripens, Lefthand may also be expected to pander to the darker aspect of the chief's nature, most commonly by arranging little trysts, or at least rearranging the chief's schedule so that late-breaking assignations may be accommodated. Lefthand might also be asked to handle tasks that, despite the chief's tough-guy public image, actually frighten him, such as rough firings or confrontations with hard-pressing creditors.

Over time, therefore, a genuine Lefthand will develop the knack of anticipating his chief's needs, to the point eventually of sparing him the potential embarrassment of having to raise or discuss any issue that might conflict with his lofty public and/or self-image. Simultaneously, Lefthand also learns to manipulate the boss at every turn, anticipating his every mood, and attempting to twist each to his own advantage. By that point, of course, a word or a nod from Lefthand can have a very powerful effect on practically any business decision. Ever cautious, however, Lefthand will take great care to make it seem that the chief is still totally in charge. And, in reality, of course, the chief is by then playing Trilby to Lefthand's Svengali.

Lefthand at this stage does a lot more than sift the chief's mail, screen his calls, arrange his appointments, and take care of the minor details of the daily grind. Now he is right into the middle of the chief's role, involved in almost every decision the man makes. Now, practically the only people the chief gets to meet are those who are nonthreatening enough to pass muster with Lefthand, and the only business conducted is business that Lefthand has approved.

Unfortunately, by the time all this has happened, the chief is often so well and truly out of contact with reality, and so anesthetized by and addicted to Lefthand's presence, that he fails to realize that their roles have become reversed. Lefthand has become the chief, and the chief has become Sidekick.

The End of the Affair

Over a period of time, Lefthand obviously comes to know the chief and his foibles very well indeed. He sees, clearly—much as a spouse does, and almost to the same degree—the harsh contrast between fable and fact.

Initially, the gap between persona and performance may have provoked Lefthand's anxieties, frightening and frustrating him. Now, he realizes that it is *he*, Lefthand, who must do the protecting. And, of course, when Lefthand eventually accommodates himself to reality, invariably he develops acute feelings of contempt, sometimes even of hatred, for the fallen idol who is no longer able to fulfill Lefthand's neurotic power needs.

Lefthand invariably makes a very good stab at concealing such feelings, but, one way or another, eventually the chief senses and is irritated by his underling's growing ambivalence. Thus, before too long, the chief wakens to the unhappy realization that he has unwisely exposed far too much of himself, then quickly becomes angered at his naiveté and weakness. Ultimately, this frustration is elevated to fury by the realization that Lefthand now actually holds him in contempt. It is at this point that the chief usually decides to take chiefish action, and the relationship invariably ends, almost always stick-ily, according to one of three scenarios.

In the first ending, Lefthand is subtly eased out of the company, normally by an outplacement firm retained for the purpose by the chief. In the discussions about the goodies he will take with him, Lefthand is delicately counseled as to how it can be *most* unwise to criticize a former employer. Lefthand usually takes the hint, fading quietly off into the sunset, there to calculate the karat value of his golden handshake.

In the second scenario, Lefthand receives a merciless shafting from the chief, who takes great care to sully thoroughly Lefthand's reputation in order to deter competitors from offering him employment ("putting some shit on his shoes," as the saying goes). Thus, Lefthand may be "promoted" into some about-to-fail division, then, following its collapse, widely denounced as a fool and a traitor, and turned out into the world with an ashen face and a matching handshake.

In the third scenario, Lefthand sees the writing on the wall and decides to take action of his own. Taking great care to conceal his own identity, Lefthand finds a way to spill the beans on his chief, thereby shaming and discrediting the fellow while at the same time rendering him virtually powerless to get even. Perhaps the most famous case of such action was that of the unnamed White House insider, code-named "Deep Throat," who blew the whistle on Richard Nixon, thereby bringing him to the brink of impeachment and forcing his resignation from the United States presidency.

In a modern variation on the Deep Throat theme, Lefthand finds a publisher for his out-of-court tales, then adds the knockout blow by going on the talk-show circuit to even more widely broadcast the Great One's all-too-human failings.

3. SIDEKICK

How to Manage a Sidekick

The vital thing, of course, is to ensure that you choose a right-handed and not a left-handed Sidekick.

If you are lucky or clever enough to recruit a strong Righthand, then by all means feel free to involve him in pretty well all of your activities, and—much as your ego might fight you—let him share some of the credit for your successes. Your other subordinates will be wise to the fact that what you do to and for Righthand is what you might be likely to do for them one day, in the long if not the short run, so always treat him like a prince.

If you should happen to recruit a left-handed Sidekick, then the first thing to do is to study your own personality, and deal realistically with any failing that you find therein, for, ninety-nine times out of a hundred, Lefthand is likely to be just a crutch, recruited—albeit unwittingly—to relieve the burden of your own emotional shortcomings. If your psyche can tolerate it, a really close inspection will usually reveal that Lefthand actually *does* very little, and certainly not too much that couldn't be handled by an intelligent secretary.

Accordingly, the odds are high that the best and safest thing you can do with Lefthand is emasculate him. If you have to do it little by little, then so be it. If you can find the will and the means to do it quickly and cleanly, then so much the better.

SIDEKICK IN BRIEF

BASIC TYPE:	In theory, the chief's closest associate and most loyal aide.
ROLE MODELS/HEROES:	Joseph Goebbels, former public relations man.
	John Erlichman, former adviser to Richard Nixon.
	Alexander Haig, former United States Secretary of State.
	Donald Regan, White House chief of staff.
	David Stockman, former financial adviser to Ronald Reagan.
FACADE:	Dedicated, loyal, hard-working, "crisp."
COFFEE-TABLE LITERATURE:	
RIGHTHAND:	Company report or house journal.
LEFTHAND:	*The White House Years*, by Henry Kissinger.
FAVORITE SAYING:	"Don't do anything till I check with the chief."
	"The chief says we should . . ."
	"You said it yourself, Chief, we should . . ."
	"Yes, Chief."
APPARENT OBJECTIVE:	To be the loyal servant of his chief.

3. SIDEKICK

REAL OBJECTIVE:

RIGHTHAND: To be the loyal servant of his chief and their organization.

LEFTHAND: To gain personal power, status, and security by serving a powerful chief executive.

UNDERLYING EMOTIONS:

RIGHTHAND: Basically a well-adjusted person.

LEFTHAND: Feelings of inferiority, high power needs, strong ambivalence toward authority.

BEDSIDE READING:

RIGHTHAND: *The Anatomy of Power*, by John Kenneth Galbraith.

LEFTHAND: *The Triumph of Politics: Why the Reagan Revolution Failed*, by David Stockman.

MIGHT BENEFIT FROM READING:

RIGHTHAND: *The Prince*, by Niccolò Machiavelli.

LEFTHAND: *Blind Ambition*, by John Dean.

STRENGTHS:

RIGHTHAND: Rationality, organizational ability, clearheadedness, fundamentally sound emotional adjustment.

LEFTHAND: Political skills, detail orientation, subtle persuasive skills, manipulative abilities.

WEAKNESSES:

RIGHTHAND: Lack of creativity, lack of charisma.

LEFTHAND: Basically impotent, indecisive, bureaucratic, considers virtually all tasks in light of own survival needs, chronic yes-man.

HOW TO SPOT:

RIGHTHAND: Administrative but not leadership success. Lacks sharp cutting edge, creative accomplishment. Most roles "assistant to."

LEFTHAND: Mentions devotion to the CEO, highly deferential to him, likely ever to have held only staff positions, seldom makes a clear statement, never takes a clear-cut position (except to support the chief), subtly isolates chief executive, attracted to autocratic bosses.

HOW TO MANAGE:

RIGHTHAND: Nurture, involve, reward.

LEFTHAND: Shun.

4

Outside the chief's door sits . . .

GATEKEEPER

The lion on your old stone gates is not more cold to you than I.
ALFRED, LORD TENNYSON

THE GATEKEEPER is the person specifically responsible for screening the chief's calls and arranging his or her
appointments. Anyone attempting to do virtually any kind of
business with the chief must first pass muster with the Gatekeeper. The Gatekeeper thus exercises significant control
over the chief, and, in consequence, what actually goes on
within the upper reaches of a corporation.

Gatekeepers may be either male or female. In small-to-
medium-size firms, the job is normally filled by a senior secretary. In larger corporations, the Gatekeeper may be more in
the nature of a senior administrator or Sidekick.

The first thing to keep in mind is that the typical Gatekeeper is merely an extension of the chief, taking his or her
tone from the chief, and meting out treatment with which the
chief would be unlikely to be in disagreement. A surly chief
thus spawns a surly Gatekeeper, a well-mannered chief a
courteous Gatekeeper. To be slighted by the Gatekeeper is
therefore also to have been slighted by the chief.

Independent and ambitious people are not usually attracted to this kind of work; thus Gatekeepers normally fall into two basic types: the basic passive-dependent or Slave, and the reactive-dependent or Manipulator.

The Slave. Richard Nixon's former secretary, Rose Mary Woods, who for a time was suspected of erasing his tapes, might illustrate the Slave. The GK-Slave is seldom concerned with the rightness or wrongness of the chief's instructions. His or her basic need is merely to serve a Great Master. The GK-Slave is thus purely a cipher who does exactly as told, and whose creed is likely to be Milton's line: "They also serve who only stand and wait." Because GK-Slaves are usually accommodating, docile, submissive, and anxious to please, they normally have difficulty appeasing people who push hard for appointments. Finally, however, they just lower their heads, cover their butts, and forget to return the difficult person's calls.

The Manipulator. The reactive-dependent Manipulator is determined to make it known that he or she is just as big a deal as the person who seeks to call upon the chief. Former Nixon aide Bob Haldeman might be typical of the genre. The GK-Manipulator is also anxious to convey the impression that it is he/she who is *really* in charge of things, not the chief. Thus, in interpersonal relationships, the GK-Manipulator is alternately passive and aggressive, being as sweet as pie to the chief but imperious and nasty to virtually everyone else.

GK-Manipulators are demanding, difficult, dominating, and highly status-conscious. These status needs often impair their ability to make rational judgments as to what might actually constitute the best use of the chief's time. The GK-Manipulator often uses the role to punish imagined enemies and to reward supposed friends. The GK-Manipulator is normally very tough on people in weak positions, yet delighted to grovel before the powerful. Watch him in a fancy restaurant kowtow to the maître d', then beat up on the waiters.

Courtesans and Angels

The Courtesan. A third category of Gatekeeper, the Courtesan, is spawned if the chief is ever so foolish as to conduct a sexual relationship with a Gatekeeper. Such a relationship is founded upon a transaction wherein money, power, and position are exchanged for sexual favors. Such liaisons are actually fairly common in big business, particularly, as you might suspect, between a chief and a GK-Manipulator, who, in the event of such an involvement, always wins in the long haul, for the chief is literally brought to heel, and, more likely, subjected to the kind of humiliating speculation that inevitably surrounds any tale of an Emperor minus his trousers.

The GK-Courtesan is normally very keen to make the relationship known to all who would attend upon the chief, thereby establishing that he or she really is on more intimate terms than the caller could ever legitimately expect to establish. The GK-Courtesan also frequently attempts to assume a role akin to that of spouse. This can be done very effectively by simply assuming that the chief's friends are also the GK-Courtesan's friends: drawing the chief's business acquaintances into detailed conversation, perhaps even pumping them for little tidbits of friendly family banter before putting their phone calls through.

Spotting a GK-Courtesan is a fairly simple matter: he or she normally dresses for the chief rather than the job, so that a male GK-Courtesan is normally overdressed, and a female GK-Courtesan underdressed. Because GK-Courtesans like to exhibit some kind of public claim to proprietary interest in the chiefish territory, they are often prone to engage in the symbolic plucking of fluff from the chief's mantle, etcetera. And, of course, the GK-Courtesan often accompanies the chief on business trips, and usually goes to some trouble to let the fact of the sojourn be known, one way or another.

The Angel. A truly outstanding Gatekeeper is, of course, an Angel. GK-Angels are blessed with common sense and common courtesy. A true GK-Angel can make a very poor chief look like some kind of divine being. A GK-Angel shields the chief from his failings, while still somehow managing to make him face up to reality most of the time. The GK-Angel is confident that the boss will do the right thing, and steers him unerringly in that direction.

A GK-Angel is not starry-eyed, and thus recognizes that some people are devilishly difficult to deal with. The GK-Angel treats these people with extreme care, keeping them out of the chief's orbit, or as far out of it as possible. The GK-Angel trusts the boss to be able to handle such people, but would not be averse to reminding the chief that supping with the devil calls for a long spoon.

Everybody likes the GK-Angel, and all agree that he or she does a really great job because, somehow, whenever there's such a being in the CEO's office, very little ever seems to go wrong with the logistics of running the business. A GK-Angel is neither Slave nor Manipulator, although under the right circumstances he or she could doubtless play either role—though not the Courtesan variety, of course, for the GK-Angel would always want the chief on a pedestal, never over a barrel.

The fact of it is that a GK-Angel is both a divine human

being and a very rare one—as all voices are usually pretty quick to proclaim.

How to Get Past Someone Else's Gatekeeper

A lot of people want to know how to get past Gatekeepers. Well, first of all, let's look at three approaches that are pretty well guaranteed to get you turned down flat.

Telling untruths. Saying that you are a friend of the chief when you are not is most unwise. Even if you succeed in attaining an audience, you'll almost certainly have to deal with the Gatekeeper again, and the fact of your deception will indubitably come to light, usually with unhappy results.

Attempting to dominate. To attempt to dominate or bully the Gatekeeper is to court disaster. The Slave Gatekeeper already has a boss, and the Manipulator Gatekeeper just won't buy it at all.

Using oily charm. Trying to charm the Gatekeeper out of his or her garments or guardianship is a no-no. Too many people both within and without the organization are already working on this, and not meeting with much success. Charm won't move a simple Slave Gatekeeper, and it will almost certainly raise the suspicions—and often the hackles—of a Manipulator Gatekeeper.

What you need to always keep in mind is that the Gatekeeper will admit anyone whom the boss would *really* want to meet or talk with. The job, then, is somehow to get onto that list of people.

The first way to do that is to bypass the Gatekeeper altogether. Find a friend of a friend in the company, let that person see that you *ought* to be speaking with the chief, then get him or her to set up the appointment. This kind of political maneuvering is pretty common, of course, precisely because it so frequently works.

If you don't have a contact to help, then you will somehow have to find a way to pass muster with the Gatekeeper. The best way to do so is to first to send along some piece of material or literature that will be of definite interest and use to the chief, something he would *want* to look at or read. Such an item should be forwarded together with a carefully honed letter, properly addressed, and individually typed. This letter should also say that you will be placing a follow-up telephone call, so that the Gatekeeper will have reason to have your name at hand when you do just that.

You should then be courteous, confident, and—above all—*businesslike* when you call. You will refer to your earlier communication, and, if you have done your job, the Gatekeeper will want to set up an appointment for you, or, at the very least, forward you to some other possibly more appropriate party.

How to Manage Your Gatekeeper

It is important first and foremost for your Gatekeeper to realize that you will not tolerate callers receiving shabby treatment at *anyone's* hands. How, with that proviso, should your Gatekeeper then decide which people you will not want to see, and, having made that decision, what should he or she tell them? Judgment is required here, of course, and one good rule for rejecting is that people who are impolite to the Gatekeeper are lacking in smarts to begin with, so it is unlikely that there would be any advantage in your meeting with them.

Similarly, any person who is unknown to you and who refuses to give his or her name and outline the purpose of the call to the Gatekeeper is also suspect. The caller should be prepared also to give a phone number for you to return the call, at a time convenient to you.

Getting this information from a caller requires a little tact, and it is *never* tactful for your Gatekeeper to bluntly ask of a caller, "Who is calling?," for the clear inference here is that any caller who gives the "wrong" name is going to be rejected by the Gatekeeper. Much better is for the Gatekeeper to say either "May I tell Mr. Big who is calling?" with the follow-up "And will he know the purpose of your call, Sir/Madam?"; or, even more subtly, "Mr. Big appears to be out at the moment, Sir/Madam, but if you would be so kind as to give me your name, and leave a message, I'll have him return the call, unless I can help, or perhaps refer you to someone else." Then, in cases where the Gatekeeper is able to ascertain that you are in fact willing to accept the call, since you now know precisely who is calling and why, you can suddenly become available to accept the call with no loss of face to anyone.

It can be wise, too, to ask for a list of the names of the people who tried to call you, but to whom the Gatekeeper did not permit access. This way you have a way of both auditing the Gatekeeper's work and not losing contact with the public—whom, like it or not, you eventually depend upon, whatever your business and however successful you may presently be.

Finally, some advice on having your Gatekeeper "get somebody on the line" for you. This may be okay, perhaps, when you are doing someone a favor by calling them at all, such as suppliers to your firm, or people soliciting your business. It is, however, *very* unsound business practice—and bad manners into the bargain—to have your Gatekeeper get a client on the line, and then put that client on hold to wait for you to come to the phone. The clear implication here is that your time is more valuable than that of your client, and I'd be very surprised if he/she remains a client for too much longer, given such a message a few times.

My own experience has been that many highly successful chief executive officers—including political presidents and prime ministers—are entirely happy to place their own calls—indeed, sometimes insist on doing so. I've even run into a couple of big wheels who actually *answer* their own phone, which definitely eliminates many of the Gatekeeper headaches here reviewed.

GATEKEEPER IN BRIEF

BASIC TYPE:	Screener of the chief's incoming telephone calls, and scheduler of his/her appointments.
ROLE MODELS/HEROES:	Rose Mary Woods, secretary to Richard Nixon. Missy LeHand, secretary to Franklin D. Roosevelt.
FACADE:	Professional, arm's-length relationship.
COFFEE-TABLE LITERATURE:	Company annual reports. In-house magazine.
FAVORITE SAYINGS:	"Let me just see if the chief is in conference." "I'm not sure that the chief will be available." "Perhaps *I* might be able to help." "I'm sorry you feel that way."
APPARENT OBJECTIVE:	To be the loyal servant of the chief.
REAL OBJECTIVE:	Often to build own status, or to manipulate or mother a father figure.
UNDERLYING EMOTIONS:	Often highly ambivalent toward people seeking to contact the chief executive officer.

BEDSIDE READING:	*Adventures of a Bystander,* by Peter Drucker.
MIGHT BENEFIT FROM READING:	*Men and Women of the Corporation,* by Rosabeth Moss Kanter.
STRENGTH:	Inside knowledge of the chief.
WEAKNESS:	Can become a hindrance to communication.
HOW TO SPOT:	Solicitous of authority figures. Likely ever to have held only staff roles. Apparently highly trusted by the chief executive. Cool and detached yet authoritative manner.
HOW TO MANAGE:	Establish honest professional relationship.

5

WISEMAN

Life is not complete until you acquire a master.
SHRI SATYAPAL JI

The Way that can be described is not the Way.
LAO-TSE

PSYCHOLOGIST CARL JUNG said that every American employer wants to hire—and often does hire—a "wise man with a pointed beard."

Jung meant that we all harbor the wish, as we make our way in an often threatening world, to be advised by a farsighted seer possessing a deep comprehension of life's mysteries, a Wiseman capable of divining solutions and showing the way out of all our difficulties.

Such a man, said Jung, "is our time-honored Mephisto whom Faust employed and who was not permitted to triumph over him in the end, despite the fact that Faust had dared to descend into the dark chaos of the historical psyche and steep himself in the ever-changing, seamy side of life that rose up out of that bubbling cauldron."

In our chaotic culture, Wisemen can make very substantial

61

incomes by purporting to point the way out of the bubbling business cauldron and off into the realm of fat if sometimes seamy profits. Such Wisemen may be categorized into five basic subtypes: the Guru, the Homely Sage, the Profegu, the Acadex, and the Commander.

The Guru

A Guru is a top-of-the-line self-employed Wiseman who earns his living selling advice predicated upon a particular philosophy. A great Guru creates and sells his own philosophy. Lesser Gurus adapt someone else's.

Religious Gurus include Moses, Jesus Christ, Buddha, Mohammed, the Bhagwan Rajneesh, the Maharishi, Werner Erhard, Jerry Falwell, and Jim Jones of Jonestown. Psychological Gurus include Freud, Jung, Adler, and Skinner. Business Gurus include Peter (*The Effective Executive*) Drucker, David (*Confessions of an Advertising Man*) Ogilvy, Robert (*Up the Organization*) Townsend, and most recently, Tom (*In Search of Excellence*) Peters.

Every industry and function of industry normally spawns Gurus. Business Gurus inhabit and pronounce weightily in the areas of advertising, finance, law, engineering, personnel, marketing, and innumerable other subjects. A quick rule about such Gurus is that they prosper in direct relationship to the fuzziness of their speciality. Thus, in advertising, where virtually nobody agrees on what makes for a great work, Gurus are ten a penny.

The Guru's past is often murky, and, indeed, he often hails from a far-off town, city, or even country. The facts of the Guru's birth and early life, like those of Jesus of Nazareth, normally tend to be shrouded in mystery. Normally, the smarter Guru in the street-wise sense strives to create the im-

pression of having been a farseeing adult for all of his life—
somewhat like, say, Richard Nixon, of whom it has been
claimed that he was born at age forty, carrying a briefcase.

In actuality, however, a close look normally reveals the Guru
to have been a firstborn child, accustomed to having his own
way, speaking out without trepidation, and expecting to be,
and used to being, heard. In other words, he is likely to have
been sufficiently indulged by his parents to have grown into a
precocious and somewhat rebellious loner.

What I like to call an "authority aura," rather than sheer
quality of advice, is what makes a great Guru. The great Guru
may point to credentials in the way of education or experience, but, for the most part, his authority is based upon the
fact that he looks, sounds, and seems in every particular to be
a thoroughgoing Wiseman. And, of course, as long as he appears to be the genuine article, the client wants to make the
necessary leap of faith and believe totally in him.

Smart Wisemen usually are wise enough to have long ago
fully comprehended this vital aspect of the game they are
playing, and thus typically devote much time to their appearance, manner, and "presence." Indeed, many Gurus really do
sport beards, and those not blessed with hirsute or otherwise
impressive appearances—like, for instance, the weedy, hair-
less, squeaky-voiced Mahatma Gandhi—normally find some
other way to magnify their presence. Gandhi did it by sporting
Victorian-style granny glasses and lolling about near-naked,
while other Gurus unable to grow hair around that orifice of
all wisdom, the mouth, frequently stuff it with a pipe or cigar
to signal contemplativeness and potency. Many Gurus emit
strange accents or offer up mannered syntactical formula-
tions. Still others hang heavy horn-rimmed spectacles or half-
moon reading glasses above the opening.

Most would-be business Mahatmas shore up their presentations with "MaHat-&-MaCoat" tactics, paying great attention to their robes of office, typically either dressing in highly conservative paternalistic pinstripe suits, or going the flamboyant route and wearing a cape crowned with a wild and woolly mane of hair, or, more recently, sporting a totally clean-shaven pate, as favored by Madison Avenue advertising Guru Jerry Della Femina.

Frequently, the Guru's garb is determined by the expectations of his disciples. For example, America's multimillionaire, funds-hustling electronic preachers often wear either shiny white suits or papal-style robes, to simultaneously promote their affinity with angels and airwaves. Wall Street Gurus wear expensive dark-colored pinstriped business suits to denote sobriety and weightiness. Advertising Gurus, on the other hand, prefer something more attention-getting, such as faded blue jeans, or, perhaps, the androgynous kilt sometimes sported by advertising Guru David Ogilvy, which was a pretty new and startling idea at the time, even on Madison Avenue. And, of course, "success"-selling Gurus like to be seen in electric-blue silk or bright red blazers, though this kind of outfit is perhaps now becoming a little passé even for them.

Gurus generally are not particularly well educated, and, therefore, most of them are quick to scorn the value of an M.B.A. or other top-grade academic credential. Nevertheless, the Guru generally is a smart fellow, which is to say above all a shrewd fellow. If he is making a living at Guruism, you may be sure he is possessed of a good understanding of his subject, knowing it at least well enough to realize that most people don't know it at all. This understanding is normally gleaned from a combination of interest, study, practical experience, and natural facility.

While the Guru as a species may affect a general disdain of

educational institutions and qualifications, many Gurus do like to sport the appendage "Doctor." However, the educational value of the supposed doctorate is seldom important, and, when they have been graduates at all, only a relatively small percentage of the Gurus I have run across seem to have attended first-class colleges.

The real beauty and purpose of the honorific is that it pushes the audience in the direction of actually addressing the Guru as "Doctor," so that, like a knight of the queen's realm, a mere greeting elevates him above the *hoi polloi.* No one can even engage him in conversation without simultaneously acknowledging his authority and supposed academic superiority.

This is a truly wonderful asset for anyone in the Guru business, the only limitation being that it is often difficult to engage a Guru in a real conversation, in that by his very nature he does not so much converse as declaim. Gurus also seldom reveal the source of the wisdom supposedly inherent in their pronouncements. Things are true because *they say so,* and they like to leave it at that. To reveal how they came to reach their conclusions might be to give the game away, in that we might discover that these so-weighty-sounding opinions are either unsoundly based, or, even worse, based upon nothing at all. So we do not query the Wiseman's word. We know that what he says *must* be wise by virtue of the fact that we recognize him from the way he looks, acts, and sounds to be fully vested with wisdom. Sure, it is a tautology, but it is nonetheless frequently just as simple as that.

Creating "literature" and getting it published is important to the would-be Guru. Newsletters, books, magazine articles, audio or videotapes represent a means of establishing authority, of promulgating philosophy, and of attracting converts to a cause, as well as earning money. Ah, yes, money. But, of course. Religious Gurus make no bones about the need for the disciple to part with the green stuff, such "giving" being held to have been ordained by the divine being him/herself, in the form of tithing. Business Gurus are normally somewhat more restrained, referring to the loot only when they absolutely cannot avoid doing so a moment longer, and then usually in hushed tones as the "fee" or "retainer."

Seminars and lectures normally form an important part of a Guru's activities, and he generally possesses strong skills with audiences. The beauty of the seminar is that it neatly matches the image the Guru is always at pains to create for himself: standing before lesser minds unfurling the secrets of the universe. The seminar provides the almost perfect forum for the financially rewarding dissemination of the Guru's wisdom, while at the same time boosting his authority and celebrity status.

The old saw has it that "he who can does, and he who cannot teaches." This applies to Gurus, of course, many of whom become prophets precisely because they lack the ability to make profits in run-of-the-mill commercial activities. However, in all fairness, whether or not the Guru is capable of implementing his own advice might be beside the point, for *his* business is the Guru business and he may be judged according to his success in that field.

The moderately successful Guru sells only his own advice, by way of books, newsletters, and clients who pay him retainers, which means that his income is strictly proportionate to the amount of time and personal effort he invests. The really successful Guru, however, spins his concepts into a highly profitable broking or consulting organization, in which many people earn a living selling his philosophy and its particular spin-offs.

Homely Sage

Homely Sage is a failed Guru. Many moons ago, Homely Sage set out to become a top Guru in a far-off city. When after a long struggle things failed to work out, he returned to his home to live modestly hidden away somewhere far from the madding crowd.

The urge to play Guru lingers, however, for Homely Sage has special experience of failure that he wants to share with others. Local young men and women, ambitious but frightened of actually doing anything, are referred to Homely Sage, and he somberly shares his experiences with them, counseling that they "can do it if they really want to," but that true happiness is to be found only in their own backyards.

Frequently he speaks in a low, sad tone, and his listeners realize that he is a man who has "seen it all." Now that he is maybe working as an insurance agent, or perhaps living off his father's legacy, Homely Sage most likely does not charge for his advice.

Profegu

The Profegu is a Wiseman whose identity is squarely predicated upon his academic credentials. Like the Guru, a Profegu purports to offer his wisdom from a unique perspective or a codified philosophy. Unlike the Guru, however, the Profegu places great store on academic credentials and the scientific method. Therefore, top-of-the-line Profegus are normally real-life professors (un-real-life might be closer to the mark).

The Profegu has come to enjoy a very special place in North American business circles. Here, where business has supposedly been elevated to the status of high science, many executives assume that a business professor must be an extremely smart fellow indeed, and, like the Guru, a resource of immense value to the bottom line. Realizing this, many professors happily encroach into the Profegu field, eminent examples of this breed being John Kenneth Galbraith, Abraham Maslow, and David McClelland.

The best way for a professor to effect the transformation to Profegu is to come up with a catchy new theory, something that sounds just a teeny bit tricky, yet simplistic enough to appeal to the lowest common denominator. Profegu Douglas McGregor did this with his famous "Theory X—Theory Y" approach to management and motivation. Profegu Ouchi did the same (and pulled off a great public relations coup) with his wonderfully titled book *Theory Z*. Profegu Arthur Laffer also came up with his curve, of course, and it was a very clever idea indeed, being complex enough to arrest the attention of conservative intellectuals, while simple enough to fall within the comprehension of Ronald Reagan.

The major difference between a Profegu and a run-of-the-mill Guru is that the Profegu normally wants to remain securely esconced in the academic world, while foraging profitably outside it from time to time. He is usually very jealous of the successful full-blown Guru, but too frightened to set up in direct competition. (There are exceptions, of course. David McClelland, a robust and avuncular Wiseman-cum-entrepreneur from Harvard, built a very successful consulting firm from one rather simple idea, *viz.*, that some people are imbued with the achievement motive, and that he alone knew how to tell who they were.)

Profegus, like all Gurus, are mindful of the need to make the appropriate visual impression, so often dress in tweedy jackets, baggy pants, and bow ties as a means of letting clients know they are both too singular and too intelligent to wear the standard business uniform. The Profegu also places great store on his individuality and "objectivity," and feels that getting too close to a real business person might somehow soil his delicate academe-developed psyche—which, contemplating some of the heavy-hitters among businessmen I have known, might well be true.

In fact, the Profegu is commonly secretly in awe of his client, because, despite all his wonderful command of theory, the Profegu is normally scared stiff by the vulgar notion of manipulating people and materials in order to make large profits. Thus, though he loves his consulting fees, he is often highly ambivalent toward the hand that feeds him. That's probably why he so often harbors notions of one day transforming industry to fit some kind of vaguely held kind of socialist ideal, thereby creating a Utopia. Oh, happy day! Oh, wondrous Guru and Savior!

Acadex

The Acadex is another style of academic again. He's the lecturer or associate professor who gets a little consulting work, figures out what's going on in the corridors of commerce, feels he can make a ton of money there, and decides to come out of the cloister for long enough to make a quick killing playing the profit game. He frequently also hopes to write a book about his success, such a tome to be his ticket back to academe as something of a hero. Or, sometimes, his aim is simply to buy a ranch and retire to a Jacuzzi.

Unfortunately, the profit game generally proves much tougher than the Acadex has imagined. Nothing works according to theory, a situation which quickly becomes increasingly frightening. The Acadex also discovers that he commands less respect as a businessperson than he did as an academic. Now it is not enough to hem and haw, to weigh the pros and cons, to make elaborate but guarded recommendations: now he actually has to *produce.* He finds that people don't get paid much for having ideas, that the real money goes to people who make ideas work. This often comes as an awful shock.

Thus, the Acadex almost always turns out to be a weak executive, who can neither make tough decisions nor effectively direct a team of flesh-and-blood people to achieve clear-cut goals. Somewhat to the surprise of those who hired him, he often also loses whatever capacity he had for thinking clearly, then attempts to conceal his inability to reason under pressure by nodding his head ("conceptualizing"), making lots of lists ("prioritizing"), and hectoring both superiors and subordinates like undergraduates on philosophical and procedural aspects of the business plan ("strategizing").

As soon as everyone realizes that the Acadex is almost completely bereft of the money-making smarts, which usually doesn't take very long, he's pushed into a staff role, where it is hoped he will do no actual harm to the enterprise. There, he hangs on for as long as he can, frequently passing his time by writing esoteric articles for trade magazines. Nobody in the office shows much interest in these pieces, but Acadex dutifully footnotes the publication on the résumé he is putting together in the hope of getting back into academe. Unfortunately, by this point he's not in demand there, either. His degree was never that good, and now that he's been soiled by commerce—and failed in it to boot—his former friends don't have much time for him.

In the end, the Acadex normally hangs on in a junior staff role, becoming something of an industry fixture and minor joke. Sometimes he escapes to an unheard-of college to regale a class of aspiring M.B.A.s with tales of how to make it big in the bright and glamorous world of American business.

Commander

The Commander, our final Wiseman, is a former service-man, thus virtually any retired officer can play (or play at) the role.

A Commander is ostensibly hired for his organizational ability. In actuality, his appeal is basically the same as that of any other Wiseman: he is an idealized adult, whose uniform, title, and bearing lead us to infer that he has been "through it all" and is "good with people," or "experienced in the ways of the world." It is imagined that the Commander, with his no-nonsense military manner, will add discipline to the company, while also helping to organize and stimulate the business troops to win on the battlefields of commerce. Sometimes, a Commander does exactly that, because anyone who has managed to rise to a decent rank within an arm of the services is by definition a somewhat superior person, if only as a politician. Also, as a result of both predilection and train-ing, ex-officers are usually highly organized people who are pretty comfortable about giving orders. Thus, many ex-officers become first-class executives.

If our Commander has a problem, however, it is likely that he will be too enamored of structure, a bent often springing from a deep-seated need to be told what to do by others, which might well have accounted for the Commander's choice of a service career. Thus, instead of being a Wiseman himself, the colonel may actually have spent much of *his* life seeking the direction of such people, and hoping like hell that his su-perior officers at every posting could fill the bill.

This latter kind of Commander is likely to make a very poor Wiseman (in truth he's a frightened child), and, at least in an unstructured situation, an even poorer executive. He can, however, often be of use in a personnel function, where he might be able to play Wiseman to lower-echelon employees purely through the rote use of authoritarian techniques learned in the service.

How to Deal with a Wiseman

A Zen saying advises that if you meet your Buddha on the road, you should kill him, the point being that it is wiser to develop your own capacity to deal with the dark or more abstract side of the world than to depend upon any kind of Wiseman for salvation. As in so many things, however, a happy medium may be found.

It is wise, very wise, to seek a *genuinely* expert opinion, and the smart chief executive will frequently do so. However, when it comes—as it always eventually does—to making decisions and taking action, to perhaps even creating a little magic, well, that is the time when we just have to do it for ourselves.

If you ever find yourself bamboozled by any kind of Wiseman, you should look right past his opinions to the source of his purported wisdom. It is not enough for him to tell you what to do. If he is any good at all, he will also be able to cite his underlying rationale. If *that* makes sense, then by all means follow his advice. But if your Wiseman cannot or will not tell you *precisely* why he is suggesting a certain course of action, then you should either very quickly replace him with someone who can, or simply take and rely upon your own counsel.

WISEMAN IN BRIEF

BASIC TYPE: Idealized adult and
mysterious sage.

ROLE MODELS/HEROES: Rasputin, adviser to the
Russian czar.
Niccolò Machiavelli, adviser
to the Prince.
Dr. Gallup, founder of the
Gallup Poll.
John Naisbitt, newsletter
proprietor and author of
Megatrends.
Dr. (and Professor)
Kissinger, political adviser
to Richard Nixon.
Dr. (and Professor)
Brzezinski, political
adviser to Jimmy Carter.

FACADE: Wise, clever, witty, adult, a
little mysterious.

COFFEE-TABLE LITERATURE: Own publications.
Who's Who in America (or
wherever), as long as he's
listed.

FAVORITE SAYINGS: "I think the key issues here
are . . ."
"In my experience, this kind
of thing . . ."
"It might be wise to . . ."

"In this kind of situation it's best to . . ."

"My fee for this kind of thing is . . ."

APPARENT OBJECTIVE: To help and save either the CEO, the entire company, or both.

REAL OBJECTIVE: To earn a living and win status.

UNDERLYING EMOTIONS: Status-conscious, fearful, money- and power-hungry.

BEDSIDE READING *Confessions of an Advertising Man,* by David Ogilvy. *Secrets of a Corporate Headhunter,* by John Wareham.

MIGHT BENEFIT FROM READING: *The Wonderful Wizard of Oz,* by L. Frank Baum.

MANAGEMENT STYLE: Charismatic autocrat.

STRENGTHS: Certitude. Intellectual and verbal skills. Creativity. Specific industry knowledge.

WEAKNESSES: Not as knowledgeable as he seems. Despite aura of authority, doesn't really know all the answers.

Can be totally wrong.
Often impractical.
Not a team player.

HOW TO SPOT: Impressive or unusual
appearance, often
including facial hair.
Speaks with apparent great
authority.
May wear attention-getting
garb.
Interested in cerebral
pleasures.
Has been or talks about
being published.
May have been in the
services, the church, or
prison.
Politically attuned.
Has earned a living by his
wits.
Seeks advisory role.
Promulgates a pet theory.
Good fun to be with.
Wants to work on retainer.
Has absorbing part-time
interest(s).

HOW TO MANAGE: Heed but never become
dependent upon.

6

In the marketing department . . .

GONNABEE

A man of small intellect wishes to get on in life; he neglects everything, but from morning till evening he thinks only of one thing, and dreams of it by night; namely, to get on in the world. He begins early and from his very youth the chase after wealth; if a barrier in front of him stops the way, he naturally hesitates, and goes to the the right or the left, and determines, according to the nature of the difficulties, sometimes to overcome them, sometimes to avoid them, or to take other measures as his own interest, custom, and opportunity may direct him.
JEAN DE LA BRUYÈRE

Real successful people have to cut corners and manipulate.
That's the way things get done.
JOHN Z. DE LOREAN

S O B A D L Y does Gonnabee dream of becoming a big shot that he can often gull you into believing he already is one.

Gonnabee looks the part and plays it to the hilt. When under pressure, however, he just doesn't have what it takes. Like the supreme modern champion of the breed, ill-fated auto "tycoon" John De Lorean, Gonnabee is a magnificent shell with nothing inside, a cardboard cutout of the image he wants to project, all style and no substance, all cocaine and no car.

You've encountered a few Gonnabees, I'll bet, for there

sometimes seems to be one in every company. Few get as far as a John De Lorean, but all can be hypnotically fascinating to watch—as people out of control often are—and nowhere more so than when you fear that you're the person who'll probably have to come back later to mop up after them.

I spend a lot of my time distinguishing among subspecies of the Gonnabee genre, and reporting their failings to clients who want me to say that some particular Gonnabee is destined to rise to the top of the company, and then lead it on to greatness. In fact, virtually all Gonnabees are *always* fated for failure. Their true destiny is to go up like rockets, then to fall back like sticks.

Gonnabee at a First Meeting

Great presentation. When you first look at and listen to a Gonnabee, your immediate impression is almost always of a tough, aggressive go-getter, jaunty and confident to the point of arrogance.

Gonnabee normally dresses for where he hopes to be going, and thus usually looks like an advertising photograph of a top executive. However, a touch too much look-at-me dash—a gold wrist bracelet, a Rolex watch, a Gucci tag—will sometimes give him away, or he may simply be just too perfect, or a fraction too gaudy, as he struts about the office, often thrusting forward his well-tailored groin, perhaps even symbolically stroking his privates. In other cases, he might look just like the man-of-the-people-type chairman of the board, right down to the baggy Brooks Brothers suit, heavy wing tips, and rumpled button-down collar.

If Gonnabee ever rises far enough to hide his non-U origins, he often cultivates and displays "refined" interests, becoming a "connoisseur," snapping up works of art that he imagines to be great, falling asleep at the opera, developing a taste for expensive wines, or perhaps affecting elaborate almost Mandarin-style table manners.

Unfortunately, the vast majority of people respond positively to the Gonnabee facade, so the type usually gets a long, long way—and much too far—on mere appearances.

High ambitions. Gonnabee spends his life responding to a Western culture that exhorts people to "succeed" first by making money, then by flaunting it. Gonnabee thus aches to join the ranks of those who have overtly "made it," the super-achievers, the high flyers, the movers-and-shakers, the so-called big shots.

Gonnabee learns, from self-help books and magazines, at inspirational seminars and meetings, on syndicated television shows and in training films, that "making it" is merely a matter of desire and dedication; that anyone who wants It badly enough can have it if only he will do "what it takes."

This message mesmerizes Gonnabee. The idea of ultimately achieving great status fills him with awe, until eventually his head is as big as that of the Elephant Man, which, you will remember, was so large because it was so full of dreams.

Gonnabee's dreams are of success and celebrity, of money and fame, of status and power. He foresees penthouse offices, voluptuous secretaries, lush hotel suites, limousines with cellular phones, finely paneled boardrooms and lavishly furnished private jets. He foresees profiles in *Forbes*, portraits in *People*, maybe even the cover of *Time*. If he's into sports or likes to be around star athletes, he might even imagine himself one day owning some kind of professional team, perhaps the ultimate American way of forcing the world to recognize that you've made it big in the money stakes.

All such things mean vastly more to Gonnabee than whatever he's actually doing right now, for he never knows the satisfaction of genuine achievement in any job. All he wants is the status.

Understanding Gonnabee

The key to comprehending Gonnabee is to perceive that he is a "reactive dependent," which is to say an emotionally dependent person whose behavior is forever a reaction to that ineradicable dependence. Thus, no matter what his chronological age may be, and no matter how winning-looking or overtly masculine he may seem, Gonnabee is a kid trapped in an emotional time warp, endlessly wanting to deny his dependence, endlessly seeking and failing to prove himself a grownup. The roots of all this normally lie in an upbringing marked by some kind of indulgence. Most typically, Gonnabee's parents or grandparents rushed to satisfy his every whim, sheltered him totally from reality, thereby quite literally "spoiling" him.

Consider, for a moment, a child in its cradle, helpless and dependent. By only two means can that child wrest what it wants from the world: it can obey or it can manipulate. In response to doting parents, Gonnabee becomes a first-rate manipulator, alternately charming or fuming, to make a parent respond instantly to his every need or whim.

This pattern follows Gonnabee through childhood. Pulling and pushing his parents this way and that with chuckles, tears, and, most frequently, temper tantrums, Gonnabee always finds ways to get what he wants.

Like John De Lorean, who lived with his mother until he was twenty-nine, most Gonnabees also tend to be slow in leaving the nest, preferring the cocoon and comforts of the parental home to the gritty frustrations of the real world, and, of course, such cosseted upbringings further impair their emotional growth. Gonnabee thus always needs someone to stroke, soothe, and comfort him, to tell him what to think, to look after him.

A series of wives—often one-time models or starlets— normally do the stroking, while advertising and television do the telling what to think, as in designer labels directing his choice of clothing. Usually, he lives beyond his means, and is often pledged to a credit-card company for the full amount of this year's anticipated bonus, sometimes much more.

Gonnabee's Anger

Gonnabee's emotional dependence is a source of constant frustration and anger, which he normally masks, either with great charm or with a macho tough-guy pose, or, frequently, both.

Gonnabee's anger springs from a deep fear of his own dependence, and from the daunting (to him) prospect of having to make his own way in the world. The anger is often further exacerbated by an ever-growing sense of social inferiority, springing in many cases from feelings of having been born on the wrong side of the tracks. Gonnabee never realizes that the tracks exist only in our own heads, of course, and so he often aches to get even with the world by beating those from the right side of town—and most specifically the rich and powerful—at their own silly games.

Gonnabee's "Positive Thinking"

Gonnabee is quick to say, his voice usually rising a quaver as he does so, that "you've gotta believe in yourself." When wound up, he confides that his own success stems from his vision, his courage in believing in himself, and the capacity to see to it that his dreams come to fruition. His problem, however, is that what he calls positive thinking is what psychologists call "magical thinking." He wants, indeed, *needs,* to believe that his own amazing thought processes in and of themselves can actually cause miracles to happen.

This kind of magical thinking, and the hunger and greed that fuel it, is carried over from childhood, when Gonnabee found that he could get whatever he wanted by throwing a tantrum. Now, in so-called adult life, he continues in the same vein, beginning with a glow of heavenly self-belief, rising as necessary to a crescendo of angry bellowing or foot-stamping.

Gonnabee's so-called positive thinking is yet another reaction to his own emotional dependence. In reality, behind the macho mask, the poor fellow is invariably a deeply negative thinker, forever worried sick about ever attaining his grandiose and totally unattainable goals.

The Celebrated Gonnabee

Gonnabee normally devotes a great deal of time and effort to getting himself noticed, which is, of course, the whole *raison d'être* of his life. Gonnabee is conscious of this wish for fame, although he rationalizes his need for celebrity status by saying that a high profile is good for business.

Gonnabees thus normally are very good at persuading the corporate public relations department to send out lots of releases in which they figure prominently, and at becoming spokesman, aligning their name with the corporate product or service, indeed even to the point of figuring in the company's advertising and especially on television, until a general uncertainty prevails as to where they begin and the company ends, or vice versa.

Gonnabee Under Pressure

Gonnabee is inherently unsuited by his inability to live in the real world to perform any kind of high-pressure management job, and things inevitably start to go wrong from almost the first moment he receives such an appointment. The reason is that, whenever Gonnabee "gets-to-be," the pampered child immediately takes over, making terrible and often infantile decisions, then, when his directives create or compound problems, angrily and entirely breaking down.

Thus, once appointed president of his own company, John De Lorean displayed the pattern fulsomely. "He has fits of anger, just like a child," said one of his close colleagues, "but the thing is we had no parent disciplining him, so as long as he got away with it, he continued to test the water even more. . . . It was destruct, destroy, call names, fight, scream, holler."

If Gonnabee manages to hang on to his job, it is always at great cost to his colleagues as well as to his own physique. He will suffer from asthma, colitis, migraines, ulcers, alcohol problems, while, of course—for as long as he can—carefully hiding such problems from public view.

Gonnabee's Good-bye

The great irony of a Gonnabee's life is that despite his fantastic (a very apt word in his case) drive for success, any *actual* success never satisfies him, and, most of the time, never lasts, either. For, whenever Gonnabee falls upon good times, he continues to suffer pervasive feelings of guilt, unworthiness, and anxiety. Then, unless something or someone is around to save him from himself, a remorseless pressure builds in his head, forever forcing his unconscious to find some way to ease

his essentially neurotic disease. The dilemma is normally re-
solved by some kind of unconscious self-sabotage whereby
Gonnabee finds some ingenious means of torpedoing his own
achievements; which is why so many apparently "successful"
men and women suddenly do such apparently inexplicable
self-destructive things.

In this respect, the ending of John De Lòrean's career takes
on special significance. Pending the arrangement of a $10
million loan to De Lorean by a U.S. bank, the British company receiver for De Lorean's ailing car company had assembled a $10 million rescue package. That loan was finally
approved, and the documentation placed on John De Lorean's
Park Avenue desk in New York on the morning prior to his
Los Angeles "cocaine connection" flight. Despite the prod-
dings of his secretary, however, De Lorean failed to sign—or
even to read—the life-saving loan documents. Instead, he felt
compelled to rush to the airport, fly to Los Angeles, and con-
clude the pact of his life.

How to Deal with a Gonnabee

How should you deal with a Gonnabee? Well, let's not sell
his good qualities too short. He is intelligent, clever in the
sense of being shrewd, good at getting what he wants out of
people, and at least superficially a go-getter. Thus, with any
luck, Gonnabee's status needs and manipulative skills might
well be harnessed, perhaps into a strong performance in the
sales area. If that's the case, then he should be promoted as
far as possible, but without ever giving him a completely free
rein. Indeed, he should always be required to report to a
strong manager who recognizes his weakness and who can
keep him on a tight leash.

If you have acquired a really high-level Gonnabee, then you

might consider making him "president" of a tightly structured marketing division. This will greatly appeal to his status needs, and as long as he doesn't have too many big or important decisions to make, then you may get some acceptable work out of him. However, *never* give him a *real* president's role, for he will most certainly therein sink both himself and the enterprise. If he says that he ought to be promoted to such a role, and that he will quit if he's not, let him go. Stand over him when he leaves, too, if you value your files.

Later, when you read or hear of how Gonnabee has become a big success somewhere—even, perhaps, to the extent that he's doing a great job for a direct competitor—reflect that *he* is the fellow putting out the publicity, and, that no matter how good the stories may sound, Gonnabee is riding for a fall, and rejoice that it won't be at your expense.

GONNABEE IN BRIEF

BASIC TYPE:	Status-seeking reactive-dependent.
ROLE MODELS/HEROES:	John De Lorean, former auto executive. William Agee, former business executive. Donald Trump, New York real-estate developer.
FACADE:	Aggressive, tough, macho, highly confident.
COFFEE-TABLE LITERATURE:	*Forbes.* *Business Week.* *Car and Driver* *Architectural Digest.*
FAVORITE SAYING:	"When the going gets tough, the tough get going."
APPARENT OBJECTIVE:	To become a tycoon, or a mini-tycoon.
REAL OBJECTIVE:	To compensate for feelings of inferiority by becoming a "Big Shot."
UNDERLYING EMOTIONS:	Anxious, insecure, fearful, hostile, angry in the extreme.
BEDSIDE READING:	*Dress for Success,* by John Molloy. *Playboy.* *Penthouse.*

MIGHT BENEFIT FROM READING:	*What Makes Sammy Run?*, by Budd Schulberg.
	Room at the Top, by John Braine.
	To Have or to Be, by Eric Fromm.
	Wareham's Way: Escaping the Judas Trap, by John Wareham.
MANAGEMENT STYLE:	Angry autocrat.
STRENGTH:	Highly manipulative.
WEAKNESSES:	Inherently unsuited to the role to which he aspires.
	Emotionally weak, highly dependent.
	Poor judgment.
	Entirely self-absorbed.
	Not truly interested in accomplishment.
	Self-destructive.
HOW TO SPOT:	"Personality clash" with former employer(s).
	Pushy in dealing with superiors' secretaries.
	Consistently talks of his "toughness."
	Often ashamed of parental status.
	Overprotected upbringing.
	Seeks demanding line-management role.

6. GONNABEE

May carry press clippings
   mentioning toughness.
May have appeared on a
   television show, or been
   featured in a magazine.
Appearance and dress
   immaculate or calculated.
May wear gold wrist bracelet
   with name engraved.
Lots of self-promoting
   diplomas and other
   "you're-a-great guy"
   artifacts on office wall.
Seeks position calling for
   "tough management."
Lives beyond means.

HOW TO MANAGE: Place only in structured role
   calling for manipulative
   skills.
Let go rather than promote.

7

The effervescent star of the sales team . . .

WOOER

Walk in with a big laugh. Don't look worried. Start off with a couple of your good stories to lighten things up. It's not what you say, it's how you say it—because personality always wins the day.
WILLY LOMAN in *Death of a Salesman*

When my client gives me an absolute no, I blow my whistle and announce, "The second half is just beginning."
LARRY LEVITT, insurance salesman

A WOOER is a compulsive salesperson whose basic product is himself.

The Wooer spends his life making people love and admire him, to which end he possesses an almost spellbinding capacity to charm, to persist, to conquer—to woo.

The Wooer's need to find people to love him affects his every relationship, so much so that it is well nigh impossible for a Wooer to be involved in any straightforward friendship or business dealing.

Spotting the Wooer

You can spot a Wooer almost immediately from specific patterns of behavior. The wooing normally begins immediately upon your introduction to the Wooer. Wooers usually introduce themselves by their first names, while smiling either broadly or coyly, attempting always to establish some kind of immediate intimacy, as if they had always been your longtime and very special friend. Wooers almost always drop some kind of compliment into their first few words, saying that they have heard so many wonderful things about you, commenting effusively upon some article of your clothing or appearance, or asking about your wonderful wife ("bride") or children. When a Wooer shakes your hand, he clasps it. Often he will actually pull you toward him, perhaps bracing your shoulder with his spare arm, hugging you warmly, sometimes even to the point of making thigh contact.

The Wooer will often, even upon first meeting, in addressing you as an intimate friend, confide more about himself than you want or care to know. His conversation is likely to be peppered with tantalizing tidbits of information calculated to catch and hold your attention. He often holds your gaze for longer than seems quite decent, sometimes forcing you coyly to avert your own eyes. Most meetings with a Wooer end with an overfond *au revoir*, and a retelling of how much your friendship means to him. Then, very soon after, a card may arrive saying how much he enjoyed the meeting, and emphasizing that if you ever need a favor you must never feel hesitant about calling on him—in fact, he's made a note to call you next week to see how he can be of help.

The Life Cycle of the Wooer

The life pattern of the Wooer normally falls into six stages:

1. Gravitation toward some kind of selling job, be it in sales, politics, advocacy, the church, or whatever.

2. Outstanding contribution to sales output, thus quickly becoming one of the highest sales producers, as well as a "character" of some note.

3. An ensuing period of hankering for greater rewards than mere money or sales status, giving rise to a push for "elevation" into some kind of executive role, and, finally, despite doubts on the part of superiors, promotion to a managerial position.

4. Short-lived success as a manager, quickly followed by quite spectacular failure. (The point of failure may sometimes be averted or minimized by the introduction of some means of outside emotional support for the Wooer, such as intense corporate structuring, or a strong administrative committee which the Wooer leads in name only, or a tough-minded spouse, or a psychiatrist, or even a right-handed Sidekick.)

5. Demotion into some kind of "public relations" or "motivational" role, with no staff and no serious responsibility.

6. A period of intense frustration, marked by the adoption of some means of blotting out reality, typically via tranquilizers, religion, alcohol or Alcoholics Anonymous, or, sometimes, a political career.

Wooers are to be found in any and every field offering the opportunity to earn a living by manipulating people through the selling of oneself. Wooers thus make their careers in virtually every kind of sales activity, including real estate, insurance, finance, politics, show business, or, often, one or another kind of church.

The Wooer and the Oedipus Complex

Like Gonnabee, the Wooer learns his manipulative skills in the cradle, cooing, crying, or becoming angry in order to obtain whatever he needs or wants. However, in the Wooer's case, an astonishing capacity to *woo*—to seek and win love, affection, and submission—becomes the prevailing behavioral pattern.

Freudian psychologists say that the Wooer's need for love and submission is explained by the famed Oedipus complex, according to which the infant Wooer and his mother develop a sexual bond that the mother subtly, and unconsciously, encourages beyond the child's infancy. This vicarious union of mother and son is disturbed from time to time by the father, who by seizing the mother's attention figuratively unsuckles the child, thereby rendering it anxious, hostile, and frustrated. This pattern is constantly repeated, one way and another, during the Wooer's upbringing, thereby implanting a powerful omnipresent compulsion in his psyche to revive the incestuous sexual bond, and therefore to spend the rest of his days aggressively beating out father-lookalikes, while simultaneously charming and overcoming mother-surrogates.

Therefore, the two qualities most vital to sales success— the need to achieve or overcome, and the capacity to create empathy—become deeply embedded in the Wooer from the cradle onward. He wants to best the old man, who now appears before him in the form of a reluctant prospect, while at the same time trying to seduce his mother, which, of course, occurs in the consummation of the sale.

The Dynamics of Wooing

For the Wooer, selling, then, *is* seducing. He beats off the competition, charms the prospect, establishes intimacy, overcomes all objections, and penetrates the prospect's pocketbook—all the while forcing the poor fellow to more or less enjoy the process. In so doing, the Wooer experiences two basic gratifications: he releases his anger and he feels a great surge of pleasure in the moment of closing the deal.

A day or so afterward, however, when the thrill of the chase and its consummation is gone, a strange sadness inevitably overcomes the Wooer. These blues stem from the fact that he is pursuing a fantasy that reality can never fulfill, for, try as he might, he simply cannot recreate the love affair with his mother. Thus, he is continually impelled to seek out new prospects in the hope of making the one sale-of-sales that will satisfy his infantile expectations. And, of course, the fact that it never happens is why, for all his charm, the Wooer normally fails to build lasting friendships or establish long-term clientele. It's worth remembering, too, that the Wooer also sees the client as his father, and thus unconsciously seeks to punish him by the simple expedient of overselling or gouging.

Five Wooers and a Wow

The five most basic subtypes of Wooer may be characterized according to their needs above and beyond status and love. Swooze wants money, Looman aches for economic security, Tood seeks *la dolce vita*, WooP pursues power, and Woogooder needs to be seen as a savior of humankind. Finally, there's the Wow, the rare outstanding salesperson who also somehow manages to stay on the rails. Let's take a quick look at each of them.

Swooze

Swooze, the classic Wooer, usually calls himself a "sales professional." In fact, he is an old-fashioned pitchman whose major needs are for money, status, and sexual adventure. He is the Music Man of Meredith Willson's play of the same name, the secondhand-car salesman in John Updike's novel *Rabbit Is Rich,* or any one of the real-estate sharks in David Mamet's play *Glengarry Glen Ross.*

Swooze usually begins his career as a commission salesman, and quickly produces truly outstanding results. Next, he goes on to win all the awards and prizes, gets his name in the company literature, and becomes a member of elite sales clubs, where he happily swaps tall tales with other stars as lustrous as himself.

During the course of his career, Swooze attends so many motivational and hype sessions, and pursues so many prospects down so many doubtful alleys, that the sales clichés become indelibly embedded in his consciousness, impairing his cognitive processes, spattering his vocabulary, and rendering him all Wooer and very little else. He is "Mr. Personality," with no real person—or at best a *very* unhappy one—behind or beneath the overbright facade.

By mid-life, Swooze might be ready to give away the whole game if only he could. He just can't bring himself to quit, however, for he is caught in a double bind: his self-esteem is inextricably tied up with being perceived as a star—indeed, *the* star—of the sales firmament: and he needs big sales dollars to support the starry image and related high-rolling lifestyle he has established.

This predicament brings Swooze great emotional grief and turmoil. His fulsome smile, like the glazed eye of the cult-follower, now masks a very dim and unhappy soul. Usually, he attempts to ease these problems by purchasing ever larger homes and ever flashier cars, or by anesthetizing himself with alcohol, or by finding solace in the arms of a series of lovers, amateur and professional.

Toward the end of his career, Swooze normally becomes highly fearful of losing the blend of insouciant charm that for so long opened so many doors. Often he will attempt to arrest the aging process by sporting a fashionable style of moustache, or a toupee, or a John Travolta suit, or perhaps by dyeing his hair, or having his teeth capped, or undergoing cosmetic surgery—or, indeed, in extreme cases, all of the above.

Swooze usually finds a way to spend or lose every last cent of his earnings, and, finally, usually supports himself by somehow turning in just enough sales to make ends meet. Often, he is reduced to "borrowing" from friends, female companions, or former clients.

Often, Swooze becomes a sales Wiseman and makes a living by instructing aspiring young Swoozes. In such a reincarnation, Swooze fills out the remainder of his days entertaining new sales recruits, puffing on his cigar and inspiring them with stories like the one of how he inveigled his way into the great client's office, how he stoked the big man's needs, stroked his huge psyche, opened him up, laid him back, got right in, and clinched the sale. Ah, yes, those were the days!

Sometimes someone might even write a how-to book over Swooze's name, purporting to share his amazing sales secrets—the first and most crucial of which, according to Swooze, is that "before you sell anything, you gotta sell yourself."

Looman

Looman takes his name from Willy Loman, whom Arthur Miller characterized so brilliantly in *Death of a Salesman.* Like all Wooers, Looman wants to be loved, but he also very much needs the security and status of stable corporate employment. Thus, Looman normally works for a medium-to-large enterprise, where he usually begins and ends his career in the sales department, doing a first-class job, becoming a star performer, and, of course, "a unique and lovable character."

After a decade or more of selling, however, Looman feels increasingly that he is becoming burned out, ever more jaded and frustrated, and gradually losing all interest in being "just a salesman." Now he wants more status than can be purchased with a commission check. The solution to all his problems, he convinces himself, lies in becoming a *real* executive, a person to be "looked up to," a manager of other lesser mortals.

After a lot of selling on his part, Looman "gets the order" and is made sales manager. Thrilled to bits, he works the candle at both ends for a while, giving a fine performance, and, for a time, is deliriously happy in his new role. Unfortunately, however, any respect he earns during this period is always insufficient to permanently support his weak psyche. Now, more than ever, he simply cannot continue to function without the *unconditional love* of everyone both over and under him.

Looman also needs to feel the surge of adrenaline that comes with what has been called "duping delight," the almost orgasmic sense of euphoria that Wooers experience upon winning a large order. Duping delight might be likened to a powerful drug that enslaves its victims to the point where they can neither function with it nor live without it. Thus, when promoted to a management role, and cut off from this much-needed euphoric, the Wooer lacks the inner emotional strength to function effectively over the long haul, or, indeed, even on a daily basis.

Looman's problems are further compounded by other childish traits, including impulsive action based upon an extraordinary capacity for self-delusion, along with a disconcerting inability never to learn from his mistakes.

In consequence of all these failings, Looman can neither

discipline nor inspire his team, and their performance begins to suffer a drastic downturn. Looman normally attempts to handle such crises by making optimistic predictions as to how much better things will be when he gets everyone "fully motivated." Unfortunately, his idea of motivation is to reach for the phone and try himself to corral the fattest clients. These customers, however, have usually succumbed to him in the past, and often regretted it. Now they drag their feet, until, in desperation, Looman either puts together some highly dubious deals that his own staff has to clean up later, or, all too often, simply loses both temper and client.

Faced with the task of fulfilling Looman's predictions, the morale of his staff plummets even lower. Having seen him up close, they know that he plays favorites, cannot make decisions, is incapable of organizing himself, and flys into rages. They also realize that he aches so badly to be loved that he simply cannot manage to operate effectively.

Finally, Looman is normally removed from his job for "health reasons," generally some kind of stomach ailment, possibly combined with or exacerbated by a drinking problem. At this point, he is relieved of all management responsibility and given the title of director of sales training, or some such. A little while later, he is either given the opportunity to take early retirement, or, like poor Willy Loman himself, simply terminated.

Tood

Tood, also likely to be a corporate animal, takes his name from Toad, the bloated hero of Kenneth Graham's wonderful *Wind in the Willows*. In keeping with his Oedipal needs and rotund endomorphic build, Tood suffers an oral fixation, so that he always has to have something—a cigar, a candy, a bottle, a joke—in his mouth. Tood likes to contemplate stuffing himself on all the other material goodies that come with success, too. What he most hungers for, however, are status and the sweet life.

Toods enjoy being center-stage, and, being genuinely larger-than-life figures, they usually succeed in getting there. Toods boast a natural sheen that springs from more than mere perspiration. They often drape their corpulence in fine tailoring, along with a nicely done theatrical accessory, such as a red rose in the buttonhole, or a huge flowing handkerchief in the breast pocket. Toods are also possessed of naturally hearty manners that usually cause heads to turn whenever one of them comes bulging and bombasting into a room. Being gregarious fellows, they normally engage in the people-manipulation side of business: sales, advertising, public relations, human resources, etc.

A Tood is a good but not a great salesperson. He fails because he tends to be just a little too transparent. He overplays everything, even—when he occasionally decides to try it— restraint. He laughs too loudly at his own endless jokes. People feel that he's great fun in small doses, but they can't bring themselves to take him seriously. He's simply not credible, never completely believable.

Toods normally dine their way up the organization. They specialize in taking customers to lunch or, if pushed, to dinner (never breakfast), usually choosing restaurants where they are on first-name terms with the owner or, at the very least, with the maître d'. Though not exactly gourmets, Toods usually like to go right through the menu, and then finish everything off with a good brandy or two. Clubbable kinds of chaps, Toods also normally belong to at least a couple of fine (or at least well-known) institutions, often serving on their dinner or wine committees.

Toods are usually as boisterously full of charm as they are of food, and, frequently, there is a pleasing genuinely sensitive side to them. A Tood has the capacity to make a nice speech, though he may go on a bit too long or throw in a few remarks that people would prefer went unsaid.

In typical Wooer style, Tood's jobs usually end in firing or demotion. This is because he invariably overreaches, pushing for positions beyond his actual capabilities. Feeling that he just *ought* to be in the boardroom sharing the cigar smoke and the inside jokes with the other big wheels, he schemes and cajoles for the very promotions that will plunge him in deep over his head. His brighter superiors may sense that Tood will fail dismally as a manager, but, being unable to say precisely why, often unwisely succumb to his blandishments.

Toods are no sooner installed in their larger new roles than things begin to go awry, in the classic Wooer style. Their judgment proves infantile. They cannot work to any kind of budget. They cannot bring themselves to discipline their staff. The classic Tood is also likely to be unable to restrain his large pink hands from attempting to explore the larger pink parts of the pretty secretaries he loves to hire (who, in point of fact, are quite often male, gayness having been inspired in Tood by too close a relationship with a loving, gushing, dominating mother, whom Tood finally comes to want to emulate).

Tood attempts to cope with his aforementioned managerial difficulties by wining and dining the clients ever more furiously. Back in the office, he will then often fall into depression, and either bawl out his staff or break down in tears before them, sometimes both. What Tood most lacks is the self-discipline to bring the world around him into sharp and realistic focus.

Tood's basic problem is what psychologists call a lack of personality integration, which simply means that it is almost impossible for him to get or keep his act together. He is too status-conscious, too greedy, and too impulsive ever to be able to deny himself anything. Add these problems to Tood's body type, his natural outgoingness, and his flair for self-delusion, and you have the basis for a very messy and unhappy life.

In the best ending, the intervention of a professional counselor enables Tood to see the error of his ways, and he finally grows up a little, tempers his ostentatious life-style, and learns to live with his shortcomings. His foibles aren't all that bad, after all: he's a warmhearted soul who gets depressed from time to time, but is seldom truly angry, or not for long, anyway. Once the expense of his kids is off his hands, much of the pressure goes out of his life, so that he can again drink and dine without undue heartache.

In other endings, Tood continues to indulge himself to excess, frequently becoming an alcoholic, then a failed member of Alcoholics Anonymous. Many Toods die at a comparatively young age of cardiovascular disease, others lose their jobs or have nasty accidents in their cars, and from then on are supported by their wives. Their kids never forgive them.

WooP

WooP is a Wooer who devotes most of his energy to gaining power, and, thereby, the public eye, along with the love and devotion of an entire community (or so WooP hopes).

The most spectacular WooP of our time—indeed, maybe of all time—is undoubtedly Ronald Reagan, who has parlayed his charm into a two-time Teflon presidency. Other well-known WooPs include former presidents John Kennedy and Lyndon Johnson, along with Senator Daniel Patrick Moynihan and Ed Koch, the mayor of New York.

WooPs are plentiful in business as well as in politics, but

they seldom meet with anywhere near as much success because wooing skills alone are rarely enough to take a business-person to the top of the tree. Business WooPs are seldom trusted by people who get close enough to see what is going on behind the bright mask. WooPs go far in politics, however, for they are abundantly skilled in the crucial art of winning votes by cursorily promoting a highly upbeat image. Thus, WooPs like Reagan, Johnson, and Kennedy, out-and-out charmers all, were well-nigh perfect vote-getting machines.

The problem for the WooP lies in what to do after winning the election, for he usually totally lacks any real administrative ability. He is generally saved by the machinery of government, which calls for the appointment of a cabinet or other decision-making apparatus. Thus, the ultimate "success" of the WooP depends upon his ability to put together a team and then to leave it pretty well alone to get on with the job of running the town, the city, the country, or the world.

For the most part, the success of the WooP is normally in inverse relationship to his willingness to involve himself in ac-tually doing the job that he was elected to do. Thus, it is no accident that Ronald Reagan, who has shown the least interest in or capacity for actually working at the business of govern-ment of any president in memory, should have become the most successful at the job, at least as measured by popularity polls.

Woogooder

A Woogooder is a Wooer who is attracted to a nurturing role. Woogooders are very numerous within the church, of course, but also are to be found in business, most commonly within the hospitality industry, running restaurants and hotel chains, or within the nursing or hospital industries, or as crusading lawyers, seemingly doing great deals for the under-privileged.

In actuality, the Woogooder, like every kind of Wooer, is mostly bent upon his own gratification, so that the promotion of his cause inevitably somehow seems to involve the aggrandizement of his name and being. In fact, though the Woogooder would have you believe that he is in love with mankind, his whole purpose in life is to live in such a way as to ensure that all who ever come in contact with him fall and remain head over heels in love with him.

At the extreme, it might be said that Lee Iacocca, who orchestrated the refurbishing of the Statue of Liberty—for his mother, he said—is a supreme example of the modern Woogooder. Others might include film stars seeking even greater public adulation by means of running telethons and the like, often, it seems, for the benefit of people suffering from the same kind of nervous disorders to which they themselves are prone.

Not a lot more needs to be said about the Woogooder, except to stress the need always to look behind the facade of his purported cause to find out where the money is being funneled, and to what end.

Wow

A Wow is a Wooer who capitalizes on his talent, stays on the rails, and remains a productive employee.

Wow is normally a reasonably well-adjusted person and a quite outstanding salesperson into the bargain. He lacks the essentially neurotic aggression that compels the out-and-out Wooer to fight at any cost for "number one" sales ranking, but Wow still turns in sound volume performance, while, most importantly, building a continuing business for himself and anyone who hires him.

As a child, Wow is likely to have enjoyed a very close but not unduly cloying relationship with his mother. Wow's wooing tendencies are also likely to have been tempered by an upbringing wherein he was forced to face reality at a comparatively early age. He thus possesses the Wooer's empathy and achievement needs, yet Wow's actual wooing behavior is infinitely more restrained than that of the knee-jerk Wooer.

Wow may still be given to overenthusiasm, along with flights of fanciful thinking, that often leads him to be briefly carried away by impractical notions. Later, however, he returns to earth, and follows basically realistic courses of action.

Perhaps the quality that most distinguishes Wow from the basic Wooer is Wow's capacity to take the long view in his relationships with others. He is smart enough to see that it is unwise to gouge or otherwise hurt the client. He fully realizes that taking the time and trouble to build a clientele of satisfied customers will be in his own best interest.

Wow is also likely to enjoy considerable self-insight, and to be armed—perhaps following some kind of psychological counseling—with a mature appreciation of his strengths and failings. Thus, he is less inclined to hanker after roles that do not fit his personality, and more inclined to satisfy his emotional needs in more constructive outlets, both on and off the job.

Finally, Wow is often blessed with a strongly supportive and highly adult spouse, who is well equipped to meet many or most of his emotional needs, and to steer his career into the bargain.

In spite of his carefree facade, however, Wow is still likely to be a fairly unhappy and often hostile person, highly prone to suffer black depressions, just like all the other Wooers.

7. WOOER

How to Manage a Wooer

Keep in mind that, for the most part, the Wooer is essentially a child who must be treated as such if he is to go on producing the outstanding sales of which he is capable. Expect him to be demanding of attention, and to get in trouble from time to time. The high cost of dealing with his problems, both psychic and financial, should be regarded as a normal chore of operating the business.

Special and continuing efforts must be made to focus and discipline the Wooer, so you should at least try to sell him on the idea of being a well-organized person and send him to time and stress management classes. You might also tie him tighter to your company by delaying his commissions and putting some portion of them into a stock-option scheme, which, as well as giving you some hold over him, would provide him with the kind of later-life economic security he seldom arranges for himself. (However, never sign any piece of paper as guarantor for his debts.)

Don't hesitate to meet all of his reasonable status needs, such as listing his name in the house magazine, or having your public relations people put out releases about him for the local papers. And by all means assign him a secretary with an understanding of his special problems.

Pay the Wooer on a generous commission basis, with appropriate safeguards, and don't fret if he earns more than your senior administrative personnel. Take care to protect him from himself by policing his sales and checking back with his clients from time to time. Devise sales competitions and gimmicks to keep him interested in the job. Reward him for special successes with overseas trips to remote and exotic places.

Don't promote him into a management job that he can't handle. Occasionally, a Wooer is promotable to a very carefully structured managerial role, but, for the most part, this is an exercise akin to cutting your lifeline and his throat, for his contribution to sales is lost, and he is brought face to face with all his psychic weaknesses. If you ever feel that you just *have* to promote a Wooer, then get the fellow appraised by an outside expert before you make any final decision.

WOOER IN BRIEF

BASIC TYPE:	Male, reactive-dependent, compulsive salesman, star of the sales team.
ROLE MODELS/HEROES:	Joe Girard, salesman, author. Johnny Carson, television host. Jimmy Swaggart, television evangelist. Ronald Reagan, president of the United States. Daniel Patrick Moynihan, United States senator.
FACADE:	Loving, warm, sincere, dynamic. A sales "magician." Vitally happy, not a care in the world.
COFFEE-TABLE LITERATURE:	Profile of self in *Sales and Marketing Management*. *How I Raised Myself from Failure to Success in Selling*, by Frank Bettger.
FAVORITE SAYINGS:	"Say, *you're* looking great." "Nothing happens till someone sells someone something." "Before you sell anyone anything, you've gotta sell yourself."

"Can I be honest with you?"
"Trust me."

APPARENT OBJECTIVE: To overcome all obstacles
and consummate sales.

REAL OBJECTIVES: To punish his father and
seduce his mother.
To win status, attention, and
love.
To compensate for anxious
feelings of inferiority,
hostility, and frustration.

UNDERLYING EMOTIONS: Guilt, anxiety, hostility,
sense of inferiority, wish
to "get even," and to be
center of attention.

BEDSIDE READING: Holy Bible.
Penthouse.
Truly Tasteless Jokes.

MIGHT BENEFIT FROM
READING:
The Music Man, by Meredith
Willson.
Death of a Salesman, by
Arthur Miller.
Glengarry Glen Ross, by
David Mamet.
*Wareham's Way: Escaping the
Judas Trap,* by John
Wareham.

MANAGEMENT STYLE: Manipulative abdicator.

7. WOOER

STRENGTHS: Compulsion to find and sell
to new prospects.
Immense charm.

WEAKNESSES: Poor judgment.
Very little self-discipline.
Unrealistic, a wishful
thinker.
Antipathy to authority.
Emotional dependence.
Self-destructive tendencies.

HOW TO SPOT: Quickly on first-name terms.
Dress calculated to win
approval.
Takes command of
interview.
Strongly empathetic.
Boasts of achievements.
Critical of politicians, police,
past employers.
Expelled from school or
college.
Overprotected upbringing.
Living beyond personal
means.
Broken marriage(s).
Speaks lovingly of his
mother.

HOW TO MANAGE: Place only in sales role.
Organize his work and
hours.

Structure role carefully.
Build in checks to prevent
customer abuse.
Give high status for high
performance.
Focus hostilities in sales
competition.
Let go rather than promote.

8

In sales while being groomed for management—
maybe . . .

FOOTIE

The most difficult transition I had to make from athletics to everyday life
was from knowing what I was going to do, to not knowing.
MARK SPITZ

A FOOTIE is a former sportsman who enters commerce
by way of sales or marketing. Footie is almost but not quite
the All-American Jock: a strong but not outstanding sportsman, an amateur who was good at his game without being
totally dedicated to or dominating at it. He got a long way in
his sport on the basis of an imposing build, good looks, and
an easy manner, but always fell just a little short in the nerve
or killer-instinct department against really tough competition.

Those who recruit Footie usually do so in the belief that he
looks so much like a "proven winner" that he cannot fail to
replicate his sports success in the business arena. However,
with a few notable exceptions, this seldom happens. Let's look
a little more closely at Footie and you'll see why, despite a fine
start in life, he generally winds up an also-ran.

Footie is usually raised by a businessman father who also
happened to prize athletic accomplishment, and who may well

have been a jock of some distinction himself. Footie is genetically very well endowed. His handsome mesomorph build matures rapidly, enabling him to perform outstanding schoolboy athletic accomplishments, which generate a superficial social confidence well beyond his years. He grows into a well-framed, thickset youth who looks every inch the natural leader and who, in a high school setting, frequently is just that: a man among boys, to be looked up to, bestriding the high school campus like a colossus, the doyen of every athletics coach. And, while generally no intellectual giant, Footie is usually no moron either, so that, with just a little shoving and maneuvering by the athletics staff, he is able to legitimately graduate, and perhaps even on time.

Footie's Female

Coming in such contrast to the standard gangly, gauche, acne-riddled teenage boy, Footie is also heavily courted by the high school lovelies, and, with more or less the entire field to choose from, finally settles upon something more than the full-bosomed beauties with whom he has enjoyed passing dalliances: Buffy Victoria, campus queen, and attractive eldest daughter of Homer V. Victoria, well-heeled and respected member of the local community, and president of the local Lions Club.

Once Footie and Buffy get together, the relationship develops fast, for each is highly enamored of the notion of a serious relationship with a partner of equal status. Already in love with themselves, they fall equally in love with the idea of being the ideal adult couple. Though Footie may still enjoy the odd one-night stand, he knows that Buffy is as good a catch as is to be found. Buffy, for her part, is very happy to be attached to Footie, for he is handsome, mature, and a leader just like

Dad. Indeed, Footie is very nearly a full-blown man, and everyone agrees that life holds a great deal in store for someone of his stature.

The High Point of Footie's Life

What nobody realizes is that Footie's day of graduation heralds less of a beginning than an ending. The happiest time in Footie's life—in terms of acceptance, esteem, self-respect, simple carefree pleasure, just about everything, really— is now past, never to be surpassed, equaled, or retrieved. Whereas most of us spend the bulk of our lives in the pursuit of future fulfillment, Footie will devote his life to the impossible task of recapturing the past.

Footie's basic problem lay in maturing too early for his own good. He enjoyed a temporary genetic advantage that made him seem a far greater achiever than he ever really was, thereby raising a false sense of his capabilities that would impair the remainder of his life.

Footie's Return to Earth

Footie's confrontation with reality begins upon the college sports field, where he is immediately pitted against individuals equaling or exceeding his own physical advantages. In this new elite, Footie gives of his best but fails to stand out. Indeed, for almost the first time in his life, he looks pretty ordinary, and is soon relegated to a B team. Finding this a new and trying experience for which he is totally unprepared emotionally, he strives desperately to recover his old magic, but somehow he can just never make it happen. Indeed, the harder he tries, the more injuries and disappointments he seems to suffer.

Things are even more difficult in the classroom, of course, where the wimps, eggheads, and assorted smartasses who were so much behind him in high school seem to have taken over the world, or at least its leadership. Some of them seem to have grown, too. They look taller, broader and less spotty than in the past, so that now a lot of attractive women eagerly seek their companionship.

Sometimes, at Buffy's urging, Footie hangs in for the full four years and struggles through graduation. More often than not, however, one of the offers of employment that come his way from people who admired him as a schoolboy proves irresistible, and, perhaps proclaiming a need to "get back into the real world," Footie quits college to accept a position as a management trainee.

Footie's Career

In the less health-conscious past, Footie's first job would likely have been with a tobacco or liquor company, probably as a "public relations" operative peddling the product to the youth market. Today, Footie would most likely be much more inclined toward a prestigious computer company, and particularly one offering "international opportunities."

Footie may well believe his story about returning to the "real world," but a couple of other irritants normally provoke his decision to quit college. First, he enjoys the seeming respect accorded him by the corporate recruiter, making a nice change from his invisibility at college and being much more like the "good old times." Second, he hopes that the move will enable him to stay a jump ahead of his peers. And, of course, another way to do that, while also plunging into the "real world," is to marry Buffy and thereby become a proper grown-up with a house, a mortgage, and a few kids. Everyone is happy with this idea. After all, everyone says, Footie is a man, really, and has been for a long time.

Footie's "management trainee" position turns out, of course, to be just another mundane sales job disguised by a fancy title. He starts out by attending seminars where he is shown how to dress and act like an executive and taught the rudiments of peddling. Footie then begins his actual work in the trenches with sales calls upon family friends and acquaintances, but quickly rises to tackling moderately prominent local businessmen. His bluff and hearty manner invariably gets him a hearing, if not always an order. He is enthusiastic but not sensitive or empathetic, and his topics of conversation are pretty much limited to what he reads in *Sports Illustrated.* Thus, as a salesman, Footie is good but not great. However, he compensates by working hard, with the hope of being promoted into management when an opening arises.

With time and experience, Footie brings in a couple of moderately big orders, which encourages his boss to keep him on the road, getting ever more valuable experience. There are a couple of promotions and some merit raises, but these seem only to involve a little better car and a marginally improved product. His boss says that Footie is being groomed to sell big-ticket items, and so the jump to management will have to wait a while, or, as he puts it, "come a little later."

Footie plays golf on the weekends, and spends a fair bit of time with clients and friends in bars, which, with no hard exercise to compensate, steadily increases his weight. One way and another, time slips away, until suddenly Footie is thirty going on fifty.

Footie in Mid-life

One day, Footie arrives at the office to find that his duties have been rearranged and he has been assigned to a new boss, who, he is shocked to discover, is actually younger than Footie. Even worse, the guy is a former schoolmate who used to be a real wimp. Now he has an M.B.A. and they're calling him a "whiz." Footie decides that the time has come to find another employer, and, after scouring the market, he lands another sales job on the understanding that he'll be made manager of the department in a year or two.

By about age forty, Footie has usually been assigned a second-tier sales management job where his main task is to exhort a bunch of fairly uninspired salespeople to give of their best for "the good of the team." Footie is not a great motivator, however, as is attested by the payroll, which serves as a continual reminder that Footie is earning less than his own top field people.

In the end, Footie quits the corporate world and either becomes a legman for his father-in-law or another family member, or, seeking autonomy and "respect," enters self-employment as a local businessman or shopkeeper. Sometimes, he may even accept disguised self-employment in a role that rarely threatens to expose his modest intellect, such as selling life insurance or broking stocks.

Meanwhile, Buffy holds the reins on the home front. Living fairly comfortably in the house that Daddy financed for them, Buffy has managed to maintain her aplomb, but only just. Her too-erect bearing signals her frustration and disappointment. She still looks good, and she's made a great job of raising the three children. She also now makes all the important decisions, treating Footie much as a softhearted sergeant might treat an amiable but slightly retarded foot soldier.

The other thing in Footie's life—and it becomes his major mid-life interest—is the high school football team that he's taken to coaching. Footie is off with those boys three times a week now, working with them, coaxing them, cajoling them, praising them, exhorting them, inspiring them, yelling at them. Making men of them.

How to Manage a Footie

Footie's imposing physique and hearty manner mask the psyche of a basically very insecure fellow, who is also more sensitive and easily wounded than you might guess, or than he would want you to know. He is especially tender on the subject of his position in life vis-à-vis his peers.

The best time to have a Footie working for you is when he is young, eager, and, still believing that he can, willing to try to do almost anything that you require of him. At that time, if you can find a way of doing so without losing him, it would be wise to get him to see the virtue of limiting his goals.

Quite the worst thing to do is to encourage false expectations in Footie, for he is only ever lower-management material at best, and he will come to hate you if you do not make good on your promises, even if they are only implicit.

You might especially try to get him to see himself as a professional salesman: not a Wooer, mind you, for he can never be that, but a well-organized, results-oriented, professional sales practitioner.

If this works, then Footie should be treated with respect and loved just for being himself. He can be trusted to do a good job of representing the company to outsiders, for he badly wants to win other people's respect, and will always try hard to do so. The fly in the ointment, of course, is Buffy, for she will continue to encourage Footie's false dreams because she wants a lot more out of life than merely his happiness. Don't bank on ever lowering *her* expectations.

FOOTIE IN BRIEF

BASIC TYPE:	Salesperson and aspiring local business leader. Former jock, of sorts.
ROLE-MODELS/HEROES:	Joe Namath. Arnold Palmer.
FACADE:	Hale and hearty good fellow.
COFFEE-TABLE LITERATURE:	*Sports Illustrated.*
FAVORITE SAYINGS:	"It used to be that . . ." "Back in high school I remember . . ." "When I captained the football team . . ." "Can you believe they've made that wimpy bastard executive vice-president?"
APPARENT OBJECTIVE:	To be an achiever and family man.
REAL OBJECTIVE:	To retrieve and maintain the level of status achieved at high school.
UNDERLYING EMOTIONS:	Insecure, worried, extremely anxious. Frightened of wimps.
BEDSIDE READING:	*Playboy.* *Sports Illustrated.*

8. FOOTIE

MIGHT BENEFIT FROM READING:	*How to Be Your Own Best Friend,* by Mildred Newman and Bernard Berkowitz. "The Eighty-Yard Run," a short story by Irwin Shaw.
MANAGEMENT STYLE:	Sports coach.
STRENGTHS:	Strong achievement needs. Affable, outgoing. Useful sales skills. Fairly practical.
WEAKNESSES:	Poor performer under pressure. Modest intellect. Unimaginative. Basically dependent.
HOW TO SPOT:	Imposing appearance, thick build, tall. Former high school sports star. Uses heartiness to impose viewpoint. Signs of underlying frustration. May drink heavily. Running to fat. Status-conscious. Dominant well-bred wife. Sales experience with large corporation. Higher education uncompleted.

HOW TO MANAGE: Place only in sales roles.
Nurture, build esteem.
Structure role carefully.
Award status.
Let go rather than promote.

9

The workhorse of the sales department . . .

BOXER

Too much consistency is as bad for the mind as for the body.
Consistency is contrary to nature, contrary to life.
The only completely consistent people are the dead.
ALDOUS HUXLEY

BOXER was the draft horse who worked his heart out for
the pigs, who then sold him to the glue factory, in George
Orwell's wonderful parable, *Animal Farm*.

Quite a few companies have a Boxer on the sales team. He's
the one who is all substance and no style.

Boxer is the fellow on the phone over there in the corner
with his head down, the dull but persevering chap steadily
servicing his existing clients and doggedly setting up appointments with prospective new ones. Forever trying to drum up
business, but succeeding only occasionally—that's Boxer.

Boxer is always so hard at work that people seldom get the
chance to find out what he's really like, and he's too short on
charm or conversation for anyone of any consequence to stop
by his desk just to talk. Nobody might talk to him at all, in fact,
were it not for the fact that he's a good producer. Although
not what you might call a great salesman, he makes so many
calls that he inevitably is able to convert a small percentage of

them to orders through nothing more than sheer honest-to-God persistence.

Boxer handles the unglamorous, low-margin accounts that nobody else wants. When added up at the end of the financial year, however, Boxer's sales make a handy contribution to the company, often putting him among its top performers. His accumulated figures over the past decade or so are probably the highest in the company, too.

Unfortunately for Boxer, nobody bothers to tote up his sales or to make a fuss over them, for to do so might upset those who fancy themselves to be the *real* sales stars, the hotshot glamor boys and girls in their sharp suits, the fast guns who like to tell of how they bring in "the big ones." Everyone agrees that Boxer just isn't in the same sales league as these people. Boxer just doesn't have any pizzazz or panache. Boxer is dull. Boxer is boring. Indeed, some feel that Boxer is kind of lucky to be on the team at all. "Oh, he does all right with his grinding away," they'll say, "but do we really want the kind of grubby business he brings in? Do we really care to be represented by someone like him? Isn't he bad for our image? Who hired the guy, anyway? How did *he* ever get on *this* team?"

Boxer's Beginnings

Boxer usually wins his job by accident. He somehow gets his foot in someone's door, makes a modest impression at the interview, and has his name put at the bottom of the candidate list. That would normally be the end of it, but, some months later, following the successful appointee's heart attack, Boxer's name comes up as the only candidate still in the market.

Boxer is reinterviewed by one of the company's duller senior executives, and comes over well. Mr. Dullman takes a shine to certain of Boxer's real qualities: his strictly non-threatening style, his willingness to take a back seat, and his delight at the prospect of joining a high-status company. Boxer wins the job.

Boxer is neither as quick-witted nor as academically well qualified as his new sales colleagues, nor does he manifest the same social pretensions. His origins are reflected in his ill-fitting, off-the-rack suits, his scuffed shoes, the enameled pins that skewer his dated lapels, the black fillings that mar the narrow smile, the row of pencils and pens in the polyester shirt pocket. He hasn't actually got dandruff, but he usually looks as if he somehow might be able to transmit it.

Boxer is mindful of his limitations, which increases his reticence, lack of empathy, and general awkwardness. He seeks to compensate for these failings by dint of discovering and then satisfying the customer's needs. When he has a sale in his sights, Boxer is persistent. When a sale moves out of sharp focus, Boxer just moves straight on to the next prospect. His major sales asset is his fierce wish to be "on the team," to which end he works twice as hard as the rest of the members to bring in the orders. Nobody would keep him around if he didn't.

Boxer's colleagues are seldom very comfortable with Boxer, for his mere presence offends their self-perceptions. They don't see him as a threat, of course, but simply feel he lowers the tone of the team. On the other hand, his presentation and results constitute a continual reminder that they're not quite the hotshots they imagine themselves to be. Boxer, of course, might be tempted to point this out to them, but he rarely does, preferring instead to expend all his energy on the job itself.

Boxer goes to training seminars, where he pays very close attention, then makes careful notes and pores over them. He then rehearses the salient sales lines until he knows them by rote. He is comforted when the seminar leader says that sales-men are made, not born. After the seminar, Boxer applies his newly learned techniques assiduously, taking special care to get and keep himself well organized, thereby giving his clients excellent service and winning frequent repeat business. Noth-ing comes easy, though, and few of Boxer's clients would call him if he never again called them.

Because of the steadiness of his performance, Boxer becomes reasonably well entrenched within his company. Though he is part of the group, he always remains an outsider, and never quite wins acceptance as a full member of "the team." His superiors, knowing that Boxer will never rise much farther, tend to overlook both his ideas and his efforts. Again and again, Boxer is passed over for promotion, either to sales management, or even to one of the better sales territories.

Boxer's Wife

Boxer's wife is likely to be the dominant partner in their relationship, often an ambitious money- and status-conscious woman who pushes Boxer to purchase a commodious home in a good part of town. More perceptive than Boxer, she re-alizes that his efforts ought to command greater respect, and so she resents his company, along with most of the people in it. She senses that the situation constitutes something akin to exploitation. She senses, too, that her husband is looked down upon, patronized. In her heart, however, she may also feel that he is not quite top-drawer material, and fret even more at this failing on his part.

In addition to her status needs, Mrs. Boxer is also likely to be a fearful, security-conscious woman, constantly concerned about how she and Boxer will provide for themselves when aged and/or infirm. Indeed, if she is at all aware, her intuitions may lead her to be apprehensive of Boxer's upcoming fate. She sees that Boxer's only security lies in his sales-making capacity and she fears he will lose this ability, for she realizes that he will quickly be let go the moment he fails to produce.

Thus, poor Boxer labors his years away trying painfully to hold his place on the team while also striving unsuccessfully to please and appease a wife dissatisfied both economically and emotionally, all of which makes for an unfulfilling—indeed, desperate—life.

The Aging of Boxer

Soon enough, Boxer is the oldest member of the sales team, but still not yet fully a part of it. The executive who brought him aboard has gone, and his former colleagues have moved on, too, either to management, or, in response to the wooings of competitor companies, to greener pastures.

The years have taken their toll on Boxer. He has to work much harder now if he is to produce even marginal sales fig-ures, and, with no clear promotion in sight—with nothing in sight, actually—Boxer begins falling prey to the psychoso-matic illnesses that assail battle-fatigued salespeople. He still works a full day, but now every day seems like a week, and closing sales has become tough indeed. Frequently at this point he seeks and finds short-term succor in alcohol, but at further cost to his diminishing health.

Boxer's frustrations now begin to turn against his employer, rendering him potentially disloyal, a complainer, a wellspring of bad feelings toward the company and all for which it stands. He may even come to deeply hate the company. Seen from Boxer's viewpoint, such feelings are understandable. He joined the company anxious to serve and with no particular illusions about his capabilities, but he hoped to overcome any limitations by hard work, thereby winning status and becoming a respected member of the team. Now he knows he has failed, and that hurts.

Boxer is trapped in a further double bind, too. His status needs stand in the way of his quitting the job, for to do so would entail losing whatever little self-respect he somehow has put together. For, no matter how badly the company might have treated him, Boxer's ration of self-esteem springs almost entirely from being part of it. Boxer resolves this paradox by staying on, letting his hatred rise and fester, and by bleeding to death emotionally, one day after another.

The End of the Line for Boxer

Ultimately, following the inevitable corporate musical chairs, a new president arrives who fancies scientific methods for appraising the sales team, all of whom are subjected to psychological testing. The results reveal what has become very plain even to the untrained eye. Boxer is too old and too tired to keep going. Although only in his early fifties, he carries himself like an old man. And, indeed, for all practical purposes, he really is an old man. The new president wonders how Boxer ever lasted so long, or, for that matter, how he ever got the job in the first place.

The president has neither the time nor the intuition to recognize that Boxer was really a much better corporate servant than anyone ever realized, so, finally, a "practical" decision is reached: Boxer will be "humanely severed."

On a bleak Friday afternoon, Boxer is sent for and told that, following an organizational reconstruction, his place on the team no longer exists, but that every effort will be made to help him find a new appointment, something more in keeping with his particular strengths and talents. To this end, Boxer is forthwith introduced to a gray-faced fellow from an outplacement specialist. Grayface leads Boxer away for "separation counseling." Then, the following week, Grayface helps Boxer to prepare a new résumé, and attempts to pump him up a little.

Not all Boxers receive this treatment, of course. Some manage to hang on in a remote corner of the corporate maze, while others, catching wind of the impending sticky end, move to a down-market competitor, or, occasionally, to some mundane form of low-paying self-employment, such as cleaning carpets with a big machine.

Either way, the twilight of Boxer's career is seldom carefree, and definitely not what Boxer had in mind. But it's always very difficult, even in our revolutionized business world, to save a rundown workhorse from the glue factory.

How to Manage a Boxer

It is most important to realize that Boxers are infinitely better employees than they seem, and very much worth looking after. Frankly, I would trade a Boxer for a Wooer any day of the week, because, treated right, Boxers both stay around for a long time, and remain steadily productive until the day they're given either the gold watch or the steely shaft. The Wooer, on the other hand, is never a long-term employee, his results are always highly sporadic, and he may well give *you* the steely shaft.

One of the tricks of keeping Boxer, and of keeping him happy, lies in educating his closed-minded colleagues. Get them to realize that behind Boxer's plain exterior stands a highly dedicated and very loyal fellow who wants to do a good job for everyone, while truly serving the team—*them*, in fact.

Boxer will never seek a lot of praise, but you should give him a lot more than he asks. You might also introduce him to some nice clubs, even try to get him started in local community affairs, or some kind of social endeavor. He's the sort who could go a long way in such settings, and this would add some balance to his life, making him a much happier person, and infinitely easier to manage.

Never forget, however, as has been pointed out, that Boxer will grow very bitter, and therefore dangerous—as who among us might not be?—if denied the recognition that his efforts and results thoroughly justify.

9. BOXER

BOXER IN BRIEF

BASIC TYPE:	The workhorse of the sales team.
ROLE MODELS/HEROES:	Harry Truman, former United States president. Walter Mondale, former United States vice-president.
FACADE:	Dedicated, loyal, hard-working company man.
COFFEE-TABLE LITERATURE:	*How to Win Friends and Influence People,* by Dale Carnegie.
FAVORITE SAYINGS:	"For the good of the team we might try to . . ." "Have you looked at my long-term contribution?" "I'm not sure you're hearing me . . ."
APPARENT OBJECTIVE:	To be a professional salesperson.
REAL OBJECTIVE:	To gain status and self-esteem by serving others, and being "on the team."
UNDERLYING EMOTIONS:	Feelings of inferiority. Extreme frustration with the company. Internalized anger.

BEDSIDE READING: *How I Raised Myself from Failure to Success in Selling,* by Frank Bettger.

MIGHT BENEFIT FROM READING: *Death of a Salesman,* by Arthur Miller.

STRENGTHS: Strong need to attain results.
Hard-working.
Useful sales skills.
Practical.
Highly persevering.

WEAKNESSES: Poor presentation.
Unimaginative.
Basically dependent.
Dull.

HOW TO SPOT: From the working or lower-middle classes.
Lacks higher education.
Doesn't "present" well at interview.
Security and status needs.
Not a job-hopper.
Ambitious lower-middle-class wife.
Consistent sales record.
Works in prestigious corporation.

HOW TO MANAGE: Nurture, build esteem.
Structure role carefully.
Provide all possible training.
Award status.
Pay for results achieved.

10

Founder, chief, and top dog on his own turf is . . .

MAVERINC

I prayed: "Lord give us a businessman for President," I said.
When Jimmy Carter got elected I went back and prayed again:
"Not a small businessman, Lord," I said.
GEORGE MEANY, former head of the AFL-CIO

A MAVERINC is the classic feisty small entrepreneur who appends his name with Inc. and goes on to create and market a wondrous widget, thereby winning what to him are life's two most crucial prizes: success and autonomy. To know why these things mean so much to the Maverinc we must, as with all our types, look at his childhood and upbringing.

Maverinc is likely to have been the eldest son of a successful and somewhat dominating father. Maverinc is also likely to have enjoyed a somewhat special relationship with his mother. She will usually have loved him, encouraged him, and subtly courted him, all the while feeling somewhat ambivalent toward her own husband, fretting perhaps that he never quite "made it," or that he ought somehow to have been an altogether better person and provider. In other words, she raises her son to be the ideal person that her husband—try as he might—never was, at least in her eyes. Thus Maverinc's underlying motivation springs from the classic Oedipus complex so crucial to other business types, most notably the Wooer.

In fact, the Maverinc is usually something of a Wooer himself, possessed of much push and charm. The key difference between them, however, is that, whereas the Wooer wants to seduce his mother, the Maverinc wants to *earn* her favor by *outperforming* his father.

Therefore, even in childhood, the Maverinc usually shows great accomplishment, along with a burning drive for autonomy. He may have a newspaper route to earn his own pocket money, and, often, in college, he will establish some kind of campus business in order to be able to pay his tuition without the old man's assistance.

In later life, the Maverinc symbolically incorporates himself, thereby entirely escaping his father's orbit, for his relationship with his company—the mother he could never quite win—is in this way somehow legally sanctified. The corporation that Maverinc creates is, therefore, crucial to his identity and manhood: it is both his lover and the proof of his potency, providing him with money, self-esteem, a constellation of admirers, a haven from the world, and freedom from authority.

Maverinc thus is a walking contradiction. On a conscious plane, he pursues achievement and autonomy: unconsciously, however, he engages in a never-ending war to beat out his father, thereby, on an even deeper level, earning his mother's sexual favor.

Key Characteristics of the Maverinc

Success in business requires more than drives for autonomy and achievement, of course. Among the other qualities that come most notably into play are the following:

A limited winner's script. Maverincs appear to be supremely self-confident, buoyantly optimistic individuals, hell-bent on success, without exhibiting the slightest tendency toward contemplation of failure. In actuality, the Maverinc normally receives a mixed life script from his parents. His mother tells him—indeed, impels him—to reach for the stars, whereas his father is at best ambivalent to the idea of his son's success, and at worst subtly (and sometimes not so subtly) undermines his efforts to achieve it. The father may want the son to *equal* him, but never to best him.

Maverinc's success is therefore usually limited. He is free to get to one level of achievement with much enthusiasm and fearlessness, but often once there he finds he cannot go any farther. This success plateau is normally defined by two elements: the level of his father's success, and the extent to which the Maverinc is able to retain direct control over the company of his creation. When the business grows to the point of being too complex to be handled by one person, the Maverinc often gets into trouble.

Intolerance of authority. The Maverinc's life is usually marked by unwillingness to submit to any kind of authority. In corporate employment, he inevitably winds up in endless scrapes and scraps with his superiors, especially in a highly structured organization. He is invariably "agin the government," and usually holds fairly dim views of authority figures such as royals, politicians, judges, lawyers, policemen, doctors, et al. He is thus not a good bet to take on as partner in any business relationship, especially if you earn your daily bread via any of the aforementioned bodies.

The paradox in this is that Maverinc is often *initially* attracted to strong authority figures, and he may well enjoy the help of a mentor or two during the course of his career. One way or another, however, he will always eventually want to torpedo the relationship, thereby again escaping from the old man's tentacles, or imagined tentacles.

A fierce competitiveness and consequent need to achieve. Maverinc is strongly competitive, and normally seeks to be the top achiever in his chosen field. He is prepared to do everything and anything necessary to defeat the competition (once again, his father in disguise), and will devote every ounce of his energy to being the "best."

Maverincs come to know their subject extremely well. They are aggressively creative, quick to spot and use any means of coming out on top. Indeed, innovation and aggressiveness are hallmarks of the Maverinc style.

A brightly infectious optimism. Maverincs are usually fun to be around. They always seem to be doing something interesting and having a good time. In fact, they show a buoyant nature precisely because they are engaged in a winning business: that of winning their mothers. Maverincs are thus always wooing and wanting to be deserving of a clientele. They personally give their clients wonderful service, thereby building their businesses, and winning their mothers while simultaneously defeating their fathers. No wonder they're having such a good time.

Unwillingness to manage a business. The Maverinc is great at getting a business going, but bored by the business of keeping it going. He would often rather sell out and create a new business than manage a static or structured organization. He is not motivated by power, and derives little pleasure from directing an enterprise. He is often a poor delegator, too, for he generally resents his helpers, compulsively wanting to do everything himself. He cannot bring himself to relinquish control of the entity that he has created, for this would be akin to letting someone else make love to his mother.

The thrill of getting it up and running—of creating a lover—really is all that can ever satisfy him. Once that is done, Maverinc looks around for other satisfactions.

A sense of restlessness. The Maverinc is always on the go, for he is seeking something that he can never quite identify. His libidinous wish to bed his mother is, of course, repressed and he would vehemently deny any such motivation. In consequence of his tabooed yearning, Maverinc is destined never to consummate his deepest desire—no matter what level of worldly success he may in fact attain. He shows daring, courage, and drive in building a successful enterprise, yet his underlying drive remains forever unrequited.

This subconscious motivation frequently thwarts Maverinc's capacity to enjoy a satisfying or stable sexual relationship, and he often fruitlessly seeks gratification in extramarital couplings or in multiple marriages.

The inability to capitalize on success. The Maverinc's life script calls for him to go one better than the old man, but not too much further. Maverinc is thus happiest at the time of working *toward* the beating of his father and the fulfillment of his mother's expectations. Once the father's success level is reached, however, his disapproval—anger, even—may cause Maverinc to suffer considerable guilt and anxiety. When the mother's expectations have been fulfilled, most of the steam goes out of Maverinc, for nothing now pushes him forward against his father's efforts to pull him back. At such a time, Maverinc's psyche naturally turns to the notion of selling out and starting over again.

Maverinc Endings

In the end, even if he sells out, Maverinc usually has some difficulty in staying away from the kind of business that first attracted him. Thus, finally, he tends to become at least partially content in serving a small clientele from a modest-sized operation.

All in all, Maverincs are decent people who make fine contributions to the world: indeed, they have come to be regarded as folk heroes in modern America. Despite their seeming success, however, they are seldom truly happy people, for, way down deep, they usually crave the kind of esteem accorded to Iacocca-style Emperors.

Thus, many Maverincs attempt to delude themselves that they really are big-league players, and, with nobody around to put up much of an argument, can become increasingly crusty and cocksure, almost Archie Bunkerish figures. Cigar in hand, the classic Maverinc pontificates on the state of the world, and tells of how, if only he were president, he'd run the country as successfully as he's run his own business.

The great irony of the Maverinc's life is that he is often finally brought down by *his* own eldest son, Smallshot, whom we'll look at in a moment.

How to Manage a Maverinc

Maverincs make very poor employees, for they normally just *have* to be in charge, and *have* to operate autonomously. Additionally, the Maverinc suffers a compulsion to be the center of attention, thus, all in all, is an extremely poor prospect for team member.

If you do decide to enter into partnership with a Maverinc, you should first take a very close look at his track record, ensuring that you and he will be able to work together compatibly, after which you must be prepared to take a back seat. Even then, however, your partner may prove a very difficult fellow to get along with, and especially once the enterprise reaches the point where it is likely to threaten his father.

MAVERINC IN BRIEF

BASIC TYPE:	Small- to medium-sized entrepreneur.
ROLE MODELS/HEROES:	Steven Jobs, co-founder of Apple Computers. Howard Head, creator and promoter of the Prince tennis racket.
FACADE:	Confident go-getter.
COFFEE-TABLE LITERATURE:	*Inc.* magazine.
FAVORITE SAYINGS:	"They can't do that to me." "I'll show them." "Get that interfering son-of-a-bitch out of here."
APPARENT OBJECTIVE:	To be an entrepreneur and mini-tycoon.
REAL OBJECTIVE:	To win autonomy, thereby beating out his father to earn his mother's favor.
UNDERLYING EMOTIONS:	Optimistic to one level of business success. Fearful of building a larger business than he can personally handle.
BEDSIDE READING:	*Entrepreneur* magazine.
MIGHT BENEFIT FROM READING:	*Fathers and Sons,* by Ivan Turgenev.

Wareham's Way: Escaping the Judas Trap, by John Wareham.

MANAGEMENT STYLE: Autocratic, domineering, impatient.

STRENGTHS: Innovative, strong drive, good people skills, highly motivated.

WEAKNESSES: Antipathy to authority impairs growth potential. Unable to cope with major success. Perfectionistic. Opinionated, difficult to work with.

HOW TO SPOT: Profit-oriented youthful activity. Aversive to authority figures or institutions. Somewhat zealous in pursuit of own goals. Self-employed (but of course). Father self-employed. Smoldering resentment of father (often masked). Warm feelings toward mother. Restless spirit.

Egotistical, opinionated.
Difficulties with own
children.

HOW TO MANAGE: Best not to hire.
Not a good prospect for
partnership.
If hired, then define clear
area of responsibility and
leave alone, holding
accountable only for final
results.

11

In charge of special projects . . .

SMALLSHOT

By the time a man realizes that his father was usually right, he has a son who thinks he's usually wrong.
LAURENCE J. PETER

SMALLSHOT is the wayward son of Maverinc, and the progeny of a difficult upbringing.

Smallshot wants to be as big a success as Dad seems to be, but the father will brook no serious rival and thus subtly sets Smallshot up for an often lifelong failure.

Maverinc inevitably has too much on his mind to pay sufficient attention to the infant Smallshot's psychic well-being. Mrs. Maverinc therefore generally tries to make up for this, but usually overdoes it and simply indulges the boy. Often, too, in attempting to compensate for his lack of attention, the father also spoils Smallshot by giving him anything money can buy, which is pretty well everything except Maverinc's own time.

Soon enough, Smallshot becomes extremely difficult and wild, which provokes Maverinc into trying to impose an all-too-rigid discipline on him. Smallshot's response is seldom foreseen by Maverinc: outright rebellion, including railing against anything and everything, but particularly anything sacred to Maverinc. In the typical pattern, Smallshot gets into scrapes with the law, is asked to leave one or two very nice private schools, and often caps things off by smashing the old man's favorite car.

Maverinc is more reasonable over all this than might be expected. He tries to reason with Smallshot, pointing out, with all the tact he can force himself to muster, that this kind of behavior is not endearing. But Smallshot isn't listening, of course.

Agitated that his son should refuse to heed the kind of common sense that made him rich, Maverinc overreacts, rubbing Smallshot's nose in his many failings. Maverinc doesn't always stop at a mere tongue-lashing, often rationalizing the physical abuse of Smallshot's person by quoting the Old Testament, "He who spareth the rod hateth his son." Alas, it is all to no avail. By now, far from helping Smallshot to resolve his problems, Maverinc has merely compounded them, instilling both greater fear and an even deeper hatred of authority into Smallshot.

The Education of Smallshot

Smallshot is finally packed off to the highest-status school that Maverinc's pocketbook can command, this usually being the kind of "college" that specializes in graduating anyone and everyone, and refusing no one who can pay the freight. Smallshot very nearly becomes the exception, however, especially after becoming a socialist and, in the company of like-minded buddies, leading an assault on the dean's office.

Fortunately, the old man is able to pay everyone off, and, after managing to squeeze a three-year course into five years, Smallshot graduates. Diploma in hand, eyes blazing, the son predictably rejects the father's offer of employment, and instead enters the world of commerce via a large corporation, determined to quickly show the world of what great stuff he's made.

That world turns out to be not quite to Smallshot's liking, however. After a brief stint of reality in the form of a boss unsympathetic to his special sensitivities, Smallshot commonly decides that success in modern business will require that he return to college, there to win a master's degree in business administration.

Maverinc's wife overrides his doubts about the wisdom of this move, pointing out as tactfully as possible that the world has changed a great deal since Maverinc worked his way through college. In the end, Maverinc agrees, and thus Smallshot gets two more years of academe—with first-class expenses all fully paid, of course.

Smallshot as Executive

By the time he finishes his education and returns to the corporate world, the acute sense of entitlement that is central to Smallshot's character has become highly developed. From day one, he attempts to live beyond his means, feeling that someone *ought* somehow to be financing his accustomed and by now patently deserved life-style. In Maverinc's absence, Smallshot naturally expects that someone to be his employer, thus he continually suggests to his boss that a person of his obvious caliber ought to be receiving much more money. The unspoken presumption is that Smallshot simply deserves *more*, of *everything*, just for being alive: the best office, the thickest carpet, the most panoramic view, the highest floor. He just *knows* in his bones that he ought never to be asked to accept an office of lesser significance than that awarded to the very small band of people whom he regards as his peers.

Smallshot is usually a champion snob, too, of course, so that, although he sometimes ridicules his father, he remains highly conscious of the status of his family's social position, and the doors that name-dropping can open for him. Thus, whereas a Gonnabee chases status by telling you where he is going, Smallshot pursues it by telling you where he is from.

Smallshot is quite obviously unsuited to get-along, go-along corporate life. His arrogance, along with his constant craving to be taken more seriously than his capabilities merit, grate equally upon those under him, alongside him, and over him.

Yet, far from being concerned about alienating his colleagues, Smallshot seems to go out of his way to show that he holds them, as all "wage slaves," in very low esteem. He confides how he is just "hanging around this dump" for the experience and the contacts. Just as soon as he's ready, he says, why, then he'll start his own business, and when he does, well, fella, just you watch out. . . .

One day, after a heated argument with a superior, Smallshot comes to the conclusion that corporate life has nothing more to teach him, and, in very bad grace, decides that the time has now arrived for him to strike out on his own and "make some real money for a change."

Smallshot & Company

Because Smallshot has trouble doing anything entirely on his own, he usually talks a rich young friend into becoming his business partner and putting up a fairly sizable piece of necessary capital. Displaying the colossal gift for wishful thinking that is Smallshot's entrepreneurial hallmark, they commonly get themselves some very nice office space, furnish it lavishly, and hire a public relations firm to announce their arrival. Then, when no one comes calling, Smallshot hits the road, descending upon his former employer's clients, and attempting to drum up business by the rather simple expedient of promising to do things that cannot be done, like promising to meet impossible delivery dates, or quoting his customers ridiculously low prices, or both.

A point worth noting here is that Smallshot unconsciously fears the very success he believes he is so aggressively pursuing. Therefore, anytime he gets near to achieving anything of real substance, he feels Maverinc's dominating presence in his head, reminding him that he is unequal to the challenge before him, provoking his anxieties, and sending him in search of some way of tripping himself up. In actuality, this whole process is so subtle that Smallshot is most unlikely to be even vaguely conscious of the influence of his own super-ego. But it will bring him down, nonetheless.

One way or another, Smallshot either finds himself engaged in costly litigation, or runs his non-business into messy bankruptcy. Then, rarely learning from his errors, his task is simply to find another wide-eyed partner to stake him once again. Eventually, he's back in the courthouse until, finally, when he's had enough of having to cope with what he calls "other people's hopeless ways of doing business," he casts an eye in the direction of the old man, who by this time really *is* an old man.

But before we get back to the father, let's first have a quick look at Smallshot's wives.

The Mrs. Smallshots—I and II

The likelihood is that there have been at least two Smallshot wives. The first would have been very pretty, definitely seductive, and almost certainly from the wrong side of town—one of Maverinc's employees, maybe, or possibly the headstrong daughter of such. This would have been an early marriage, perhaps even when Smallshot was still at college. The little lovely—perhaps a Gladys or a Rose—would have been attracted by Smallshot's rebellious nature, his fondness for a good time, his ready cash, and, of course, his off-limits social status. Smallshot's feelings for her require no explanation. This kind of marriage usually lasts, at most, a couple of years.

Smallshot's second wife—probably a Buffy or a Muffy— would be a different breed of cat altogether: well bred, status-conscious, chiseled-straight-Jane-style attractive, and always meticulously turned out. They both marry for status, yet each hopes that somehow their union might also yield large financial blessings. Her particular understanding and desire is that even if he should fail to enter the family business, he will still at least accept his share of the family fortune when Maverinc finally casts off from this mortal coil.

Such a union normally brings forth two lovely children, Smallshot II and Wendy or Pamela. The Smallshots choose a large but tasteful home in a nice little suburb, not too far from a prestigious country club. She raises the children, plays some light tennis, does a little volunteer work at the local hospital, and, increasingly, with the passage of time, fumes.

Wanting so much more in the way of status and money, yet realizing that Smallshot is never going to make it on his own, Buffy/Muffy is finally very relieved when her husband ultimately agrees—as he usually does—to accept employment in the family firm. And, indeed, she may by then very well have secretly engineered the offer.

The Return of the Prodigal Son

With faint fanfare and two reluctant cheers from the employees, Smallshot joins the family firm, most likely as vice-president in charge of administration. He is, however, not an instant success in this role, his management style proving to be something of a burden for everyone. Initially, he attempts to assert himself, to win respect, and to hide his chronic dependence by attempting to emulate his father and adopting a highly autocratic, don't-argue-with-me approach. Then, when things go wrong for Smallshot, which is most of the time, he simply flies into a rage.

The end of the line comes when Maverinc wisely sells out to a large conglomerate. After taking a close look at Smallshot, the new owner relegates him to his final position, vice-president in charge of special projects, reporting directly to the executive vice-president, a fairly switched-on fellow who can see some virtue in keeping Smallshot around for just as long as Maverinc is prepared to hang on in his new role as "chairman of the executive committee."

Why Smallshot Goes off the Rails

Smallshot is spoiled, immature, angry, manipulative, and out of touch with reality. Like Gonnabee, he too is a *reactive-dependent* who spends his "adult" life responding to his unfortunate upbringing.

There is, however, a slight but crucial difference in their motivations. Whereas Gonnabee is out to prove himself better than everybody, Smallshot's psychic commitment is to show that he is as good as the old man. Unfortunately for Smallshot this is still a very tall order, since, as we have seen, he lacks his father's blend of charm, nerve, push, cunning, energy, and perseverance.

Smallshot normally nurses his failure in his contest with his father well into mid-life, and often into old age, always running against the fear that he will fail to meet Maverinc's standards, continually raging against his "unfair" upbringing, and always seeking ways of getting even, while—since these processes are all unconscious—never having the slightest notion of the unique set of problems that conspires to confound him.

What to Do with a Smallshot

It is very hard to assist Smallshots since they are seldom prepared to acknowledge or discuss either the cause or the extent of their problems. They really need a lot of help, including professional therapy, but the chances of getting Smallshot to recognize this fact—or if he goes at all, to make any sincere attempt to profit from therapy—are fairly slight.

The best thing to do with a Smallshot, then, is to get him away from the family firm, thereby making him suffer the consequences of his own failings in the hope that he may one day begin to awaken, and, through that painful process, grow up to a greater or lesser extent.

Alternatively, you might ease or force him into some area of employment that offers a little status but no real responsibility, and ideally something that allows you both to capitalize upon his father's reputation and connections, which, as long as Smallshot fails to develop any self-insight, are his only major assets.

SMALLSHOT IN BRIEF

BASIC TYPE:	Son of the founder of a medium-sized successful business. A reactive dependent.
ROLE MODELS/HEROES:	Rupert Murdoch, media magnate. Henry Ford II, auto executive.
FACADE:	Arrogant, tough, macho, highly confident.
COFFEE-TABLE LITERATURE:	Country club membership directory. *Town and Country* magazine. *The Rise and Decline of the Roman Empire,* by Arnold J. Toynbee.
FAVORITE SAYINGS:	"Business is much more sophisticated, these days." "I'm not gonna get mad, I'm gonna get even."
APPARENT OBJECTIVE:	To become a tycoon.
REAL OBJECTIVES:	To prove he's better than the old man. To compensate for feelings of inferiority.

UNDERLYING EMOTIONS:	Anxious, insecure, fearful, extremely hostile.
BEDSIDE READING:	*Fathers and Sons,* by Ivan Turgenev.
MIGHT BENEFIT FROM READING:	*Scripts People Live,* by Claude Steiner. *Wareham's Way: Escaping the Judas Trap,* by John Wareham.
MANAGEMENT STYLE:	Autocratic.
STRENGTHS:	Manipulative, driven.
WEAKNESSES:	Extremely poor judgment. Unrealistic, a wishful thinker. Refuses to accept authority. Highly dependent. Self-destructive.
HOW TO SPOT:	Black sheep of well-to-do family. Father a successful businessman. Highly ambitious. Critical of politicians, police, past employers. Expelled from school or college. Overindulged upbringing. Living beyond personal means. Broken marriage(s).

11. SMALLSHOT

HOW TO MANAGE: Place in high-status low-
supervisory role.
Get him professional help.
Let go rather than promote.

12

Crunching numbers or counting beans . . .

BOYSCOUT

Be prepared.
BOY SCOUT MOTTO

AT A TIDY DESK in the corner of the planning department, an old-fashioned slide rule in his hand, five felt-tip pens and two sharp pencils poking out of his shirt pocket, peering through thick lenses, lost in thought, sits Boyscout.

There were high hopes for Boyscout when he applied to the company as a management trainee, fresh out of a fairly reasonable college with two degrees, the master's with honors, and a solid record in serious-minded, slightly left-wing campus activities. He'd come across well in the interview and had done his homework on the company, knowing the questions to ask, and asking them in a sober and sophisticated fashion. "No doubt about it," said George of personnel, "he's an achiever, got a ton of potential. With a little seasoning, he could really make a big difference around here. A *big* difference, mark my words."

Some ten years and three demotions later, Boyscout has found his niche. Hair now silvering at the sides, yet still somehow managing to seem both youthful and serious, Boyscout works as an assistant in the strategic planning department, where he assembles the five-year budget forecasts. Someone else will look them over later, just to ensure that everything makes sense.

Boyscout is not entirely happy with his job, but he likes the security that it provides. When bored, he daydreams about joining some other big corporation, serving a charismatic leader, and remaking the world. This will not happen, however, for something is wrong with Boyscout. Everyone agrees on that, yet no one quite seems to know what it is, or what precisely went amiss with his career.

The Trouble with Boyscout

The nub of Boyscout's problem, and of his subsequent failure, is that, like Gonnabee and so many others, he is another one of those people who never grow up. Throughout adolescence, and especially during college, he often seemed a lot older than his years, so much so that sometimes he seemed not so much precocious as prematurely set in his thinking, altogether too serious, too prudent, too cautious. The reality, however, is that Boyscout never got beyond the emotional age of about thirteen.

One of the reasons that even sophisticated people have difficulty in spotting Boyscout's innate immaturity is that they associate immaturity with the carefree charm of the Wooer-style personality, and there is none of that with Boyscout. Where Wooer is childlike, mischievous, and engaging, Boyscout is decent, earnest, pious, humorless, and as conventional as the home from which he sprang. Since, as with the entire species *Homo sapiens*, his upbringing holds the key to his personality, let's look a little more closely at his childhood.

The Making of Boyscout

Lower-middle-class parents raised Boyscout first and foremost to obey. Next, they taught him to prize conformity and upward striving. After that, they admonished that the best way to master a threatening world is to be a good boy, work hard, acquire knowledge, and serve a worthy master, just like Dad. That way, they counseled him, those in authority will look after you, and you'll stay out of trouble.

The family home, though not unhappy, provoked a faint sense of anxiety regarding the need to make one's way in the world. Boyscout was advised to be frugal, careful, prudent, patient, and painstaking. He was cautioned to strive, but not to aspire beyond his station. Taught to respect and fear authority, he came to believe that those in power got there as a result of some kind of magisterial master plan, probably God's. All of this left him a little confused.

Boyscout will almost certainly actually have *been* a Boy Scout; either that or a Jaycee, or both. To be certain, he will have been a member of a conformist church that evangelizes the goals of self-improvement and community service. To this end, he probably took up football, distance running, or wrestling: something to improve his body, involve him with others, and punish him, thus assuaging the guilt that is so much a part of his makeup.

Boyscout embraces his religion keenly, finding peace in a piety that promises certainty of purpose in this world, plus salvation in the next. He is also attracted by religious trappings: the smells, the bells, the robes, the hierarchical nature and solemnity and panoply of the thing. No matter his particular subcreed, he is a muscular Christian, the kind of person enamored by the notion, if not the reality, of dying for an ideal that is not quite clear to him.

He also cherishes a vague appreciation for things aesthetic, enjoying perhaps sacred or orchestral music, visiting galleries, subscribing to a literary club that mails him a "collector's" series of leather-bound classics.

Taught to value cerebral accomplishment, and hoping to compensate for his lack of innate perception, Boyscout greatly prizes education and thus studies assiduously. Deep down, he hopes to solve the many anxiety-provoking riddles of life in general and his in particular by reading books, passing examinations, and winning diplomas. Intending to obtain the "right" programming for his career, he typically completes at least one technical qualification or degree, and often goes on to pursue a master's, or a doctorate. In the end, however, no matter how many diplomas he gathers up, he still worries that he never *quite* got to the center of things, and wishes that he could study even further in order to become as smart as his role models, whose ranks he unconsciously knows he has not attained, and whose exalted status he fears he will never reach.

Mrs. Boyscout

Boyscout will probably meet his future spouse while singing in the church choir, a rendezvous made in heaven, they both may feel. She inevitably is his mother in disguise, and it is seldom a good disguise. Somewhat older than Boyscout, she will certainly be dominating, and probably a plump endomorph, stout of heart, short of limb, large of breast, round of belly, and wide of hip, all the better to raise a family, and to wear a stout pair of pants.

She will have been attracted by Boyscout's submissive nature along with his naiveté, vulnerability, general uprightness, and seeming good value. He might not be Don Juan, but he will be a solid provider, or so her unconscious thought processes will have her believe. Sharing his religious bent, she will settle down with him to build a snug nest and populate it with fine progeny.

All in all, Mr. and Mrs. Boyscout are fairly well suited to their relationship. His normal response to pressure is to retreat into himself, so they rarely argue. Inherently passive and submissive, he enjoys the emotional security of having his loved one tell him how to behave. On Sunday evenings, he may even be permitted the succor of her warm body, a perhaps pleasant change from his punishing sports.

Boyscout on the Job

During the week, Boyscout loves his master, his manual, his code, and his uniform. He likes large, highly structured companies where advancement is determined strictly by seniority. He hopes to ascend the corporate hierarchy by serving time, earning badges, looking the part, getting years of service on his sleeve, and being prepared.

Boyscout's short-cropped hair is neatly in place. His company tie, discreetly knotted and worn with pride, sits just below his Adam's apple. His slightly out-of-style solid gray suit is well pressed. His pants, two inches too short, expose patterned socks that are also too short. His prep-school-style wing tips are brightly shined, especially the backs. The laces are double-knotted, a precaution against being tripped. The papers in his briefcase, very neatly arranged, nestle next to the company manual and the lunch he makes for himself each morning. He may also carry a pocket chess set, a lap computer, a map of the city, spare bus tokens, a plastic raincoat with a foldout hood, a Swiss army pocketknife, and a prayerbook. He is ready for anything, including the Valley of Death.

Boyscout's prime motivation is, of course, to do good, serve others, and become a decent and accepted member of the community whose approval means so much to him. Both his idealism and his upbringing make him hanker to do something big and clean, but two conflicting needs inhibit these fine intentions. First, there is his tremendous need for structure, the result of which is that in order to actually accomplish anything, he must always be told *exactly* how to do it. Second, there is his equal need for economic and emotional security beyond that provided by his spouse. Thus, even though he likes the idea of adventure, he is frightened to take even the smallest of risks that might lead to it.

Boyscout: Intelligent Yet Somewhat Silly

Boyscout's natural intelligence is highly developed. He is quick to analyze solid forms, can solve puzzles, tie knots, play chess, fix a bicycle. If lost on an expedition, he could survive—for a while, anyway—on berries and roots. He can perform any task listed in his manual, plus nearly anything else in which he has been thoroughly instructed, for when it comes to following detailed instructions to the letter, he has no peer.

What Boyscout cannot ever do, however, is think for himself. He is so hopelessly naive that you might be forgiven for assuming that part of his brain is missing. He knows how to forecast the weather, yet, in the absence of an order, would generally never dream of coming in out of the rain.

What Boyscout really wants to do, even in so-called adult life, is to continue to serve a trustworthy and competent scout leader: someone who, working from a well-defined master plan, will devise a moderately difficult yet always attainable and reasonably fulfilling undertaking. Boyscout wants to be tested, but he wants his testing to be "fair." He wants to feel

155

that as long as he does his homework and his prescribed exercises, all will go swimmingly for him.

Thus, Boyscout always welcomes instruction from his boss, and receives it standing earnestly erect, head turned to one side, ear cocked, highly attentive and anxious only that the orders be crystal clear in every detail. "Gotcha, Chief," he says, when they are. "Yep, gotcha, Chief. Right away, Chief."

Boyscout Is Impotent

Boyscout is a hard worker who feels intensely guilty whenever he believes he may have sinned by failing to do his very best. He also tends to value the processes of working hard and attending to detail more highly than their effectiveness, so that, despite his genuinely good intentions, he is usually slow in getting things done. Much of that time is spent organizing his week, then his day, then his desk, then his mind: he sharpens pencils, makes checklists, and draws impeccable flow charts. Yet, somehow, sadly, things rarely come out as planned.

A central problem is that Boyscout literally cannot think under pressure. Wanting desperately to be seen as a good boy while simultaneously fearing the wrath of God, he frets terribly whenever an unforeseen situation or problem calls for a nonmanualized or visceral reaction, or, worse yet, a solution. Thus, in the face of such predicaments, he either buries himself in detail or freezes into immobility.

Boyscout is prone, too, to long-windedness, and is often unable to come to the point when attempting to explain himself. He is uncomfortable telling others what he is doing, for this often runs counter to his values, and he also fears that he might be blamed for saying the wrong thing. He much prefers it when people tell *him* what to do, then, when things go wrong, as they frequently do, he seeks to be spared all blame, saying, "I was only following orders"—which is totally true, of course.

No matter how intelligent or well educated Boyscout may be, his approach to real-life problems is superficial. Every problem is like a Gordian knot that he can apprehend yet not comprehend. He reaches for solutions, but is always left poking the air, never able to come up with anything of substance. Somehow, whenever he is in charge, everything just seems to fall through the cracks.

Boyscout as Leader

If asked to lead or direct a group, Boyscout's management style is that of the scout leader or missionary. He recruits docile subordinates, then mothers them. If they are submissive enough, they might enjoy this for a while, but, in the clutch, they will eventually grow fearful and run to someone stronger. Anxious to dogmatize his underlings as he has himself, he will preach to them from the company manual, or even an organizational code of ethics that he has personally drafted, or caused to be drafted. He will issue close instructions to those under him, and then go on to monitor the detail of their work. Feeling guilty in the role of boss, he takes great trouble to treat everyone fairly. He may share the duties of his unit, in an effort to have its members feel that he is one of the team rather than its leader. When things go wrong, as they always do for him, he frets, freezes, dithers, then, finally, looks for—and often prays for—the intervention of a greater authority.

Boyscouts and Eaglescouts

A distinction must be made between Boyscouts and Eaglescouts. Eaglescouts are the top of the line. Eaglescouts are serious fellows, intensely zealous in their approach to all tasks, and much given to weighty discussions on styles of leadership. They are highly qualified, often possessing doctorates, or even prestigious good-boy awards such as Rhodes or Fulbright scholarships, and they are usually "snapped up" out of college by inexperienced corporate recruiters dazzled by all of this superficial weightiness.

Eaglescouts almost always join large multinational organizations, ostensibly hoping to improve the world and do good for all of humankind. In actuality, however, even though the Eaglescout may initially be given a place on the fast track, or even pushed straight up to a genuine line position, he never pans out in the end. After failing, he is quietly separated from real power, shunted into various do-gooder activities, and left to gather dust in a quiet corner.

Feeling that he has been shortchanged, yet knowing in his heart that he has not, the middle-aged Eaglescout hangs onto the money (he is always overpaid), while developing a patronizing resentment toward the hand that feeds him. Thus, he typically both despises and envies the genuinely successful entrepreneur, believing him to be an intellectual lightweight, while remaining blind to the real sources of success that he himself would so much like to emulate.

The important thing to understand about the Eaglescout is that, no matter how dazzling his qualifications, credentials, badges, diplomas, etc., he is and forever will remain naive, insecure, and unable to perform in any but a highly structured role, for he can only ever do what he has been told to do— and not always that, and not always terribly well when he does.

How to Deal with a Boyscout

It is primarily greed that causes people to promote Boyscout to a job he cannot handle. Employers fall prey to the wish to hire such people in order to profit handsomely from their supposed high technical qualifications and overflowing zeal. "There *must* be some way we can use this fine fellow," they say. And there is, of course. It is just a matter of lowering expectations.

Boyscouts are great in any job calling for hard work, perseverance, logical (as opposed to intuitive) analytical skills, attention to detail, eagerness to work within a clear-cut structure, and the opportunity to feel that they are making useful contributions to the team, and also, ideally, humankind.

Boyscouts make good team players, sound backroom boys, wonderful legal proofreaders, first-class auditors and accountants, and moderately good gofers. They can be relied upon to follow orders to the letter, if not always the intent.

The surest way to keep your Boyscout happy is to reward him with sermonlike praise, together with letters of congratulation, and pretty certificates. Actual money in the form of modest merit increases might not go amiss either, but this need not be overdone. It is best to convince him, if possible— and this shouldn't be too hard—that his real reward is the contribution that he is making to others.

Never, of course, put Boyscout in charge of anything demanding imagination or intuition, and seldom pay much heed to his judgment. Boyscouts are decent people who deserve to be looked after, but you shouldn't load yourself down with too many of them, nor ever take them as seriously as they take themselves.

BOYSCOUT IN BRIEF

BASIC TYPE:	Overqualified clerk or bureaucrat.
ROLE MODELS/HEROES:	Jimmy Carter, former United States president. Josh Miner, founding trustee of Outward Bound in the United States. Edward Heath, former British prime minister.
FACADE:	Dedicated, loyal, hard-working, go-getting company man.
COFFEE-TABLE LITERATURE:	*Discover* magazine.
FAVORITE SAYINGS:	"What is the game plan, exactly?" "The book says we have to . . ." "Surely we cannot make exceptions?"
APPARENT OBJECTIVE:	To serve a great company or a fine master.
REAL OBJECTIVE:	To be saved from an apparently threatening world.
UNDERLYING EMOTIONS:	Fearful, insecure, pious, extremely low tolerance for ambiguous situations. Resentful in later life.

12. BOYSCOUT

BEDSIDE READING: The complete works of Norman Vincent Peale.

MIGHT BENEFIT FROM READING: *Extraordinary Popular Delusions and the Madness of Crowds,* by Charles MacKay.
Escape from Freedom, by Eric Fromm.
The Organization Man, by William White.

MANAGEMENT STYLE: Missionary or scout leader.

STRENGTHS: Strong achievement needs.
Technically well qualified.
Highly educated.
Wants to be a "team player."

WEAKNESSES: Impotent.
Neither a leader nor possessing leadership material.
Naive in the extreme.
Cannot really think for himself.

HOW TO SPOT: Overeducated.
Works for large, highly structured organization.
Religious, pious.
Attracted to punishing athletic sports.

Spouse the dominant
  partner.
Spouse older than Boyscout.
Highly perfectionistic.
Conformist upbringing.
Parents lower-middle-class.

HOW TO MANAGE: Structure the job tightly.
Put into staff role.
Exploit technical expertise.

13

That tough new cookie down the hall . . .

SUPERGIRL

There was a little girl who had a little curl
Right in the middle of her forehead.
When she was good, she was very very good,
But when she was bad she was horrid.
NURSERY RHYME

YOU'VE NO DOUBT seen a Supergirl or two featured
in magazine articles, or on the television talk shows.

She's the apparently tough and seemingly very successful
businesswoman who is breathlessly cited as having *made it in
a man's world,* and who is now involved in the happy process
of having it all and telling it all.

After relating her Horatio Alger tale, she normally goes on
to proffer pointers to other females intent upon emulating her
success. Some enterprising publisher may even put her name
to a book telling her "inside story."

As a prospective employer, the first thing to note about Supergirl is that, despite her well-tailored conservative suit and
expensive leather briefcase, and despite all those vaunted
"achievements" and all that charm, she is much more girl than
super—which is to say that she can *play* at being an executive,
but never truly *be* one.

Supergirl is actually another spoiled child, very much in the mold of our old friend Gonnabee. She is charming in the pursuit of what she wants, but becomes mean and angry whenever she cannot get it. She feels that she is some kind of "star," and therefore entitled to behave like a prima donna. As Muhammad Ali once noted, however, any right to play prima donna comes from being able to perform like one—day in and day out, year after year, to the delight of critics, public, peers, and colleagues—and Supergirl certainly cannot do that, nor, for that matter, ever get near to doing it.

Close scrutiny inevitably also reveals that Supergirl simply cannot make good on her claims of having succeeded in the upper reaches of management where the real men live (and the real women, too, of course, but Supergirl would think only of the men).

In other words, Supergirl is an out-and-out manipulator rather than a manager, most of her so-called "successes" springing from what she would likely call "salespersonship." What this means is that, like most salespeople, Supergirl spends much of her life attempting to make people fall in love with her, and often succeeding. Also, like most salespeople, Supergirl is possessed of an apparently enormous yet highly fragile ego that renders her inherently unsuited to hold any senior executive position, no matter how effective a role-player she might seem. She is no Indira Gandhi, no Margaret Thatcher, and no Elizabeth Dole; neither is she even a Rosalynn Carter or a Nancy Reagan. No, unlike these tough-minded, hard-nosed, capable *women*, Supergirl is a girl, and only a girl, as is clearly to be discovered from peeking into her past.

The Making of Supergirl

Supergirl is usually the eldest child, and often the only child, of a sonless marriage. Her initally disappointed but later doting father teaches her to go after the things he wanted for himself. Like most men, he usually wanted a lot more out of life than he ever got, and so now he hopes to win admiration and credit through amazing feats to be performed by his prodigious daughter. He tells her that she is just as good as any fellow, and instills in her the need to become a "success," by which he normally means first to make a lot of money and then to make sure that a lot of people know about it. To this end, her father becomes her guide and mentor, charting her progress and reinforcing her successes—or imagined successes—with lavish praise, while conveniently entirely ignoring her failures. Daddy tells neighbors, friends, grandparents, schoolteachers—and, of course, Supergirl herself—that "my daughter is *amazing*, just as good as any boy and better than most." And he believes it, too, of course—or at least for a while.

Supergirl's mother is usually a pleasant woman, content to occupy a back seat in the relationship between father and daughter. However, the mother does have a role: that of Supergirl's *antimodel*, or "just a housewife." Supergirl is told by Daddy that Mommy was a victim of her upbringing, and that, whatever else Supergirl may do, she should stay out of that trap at all cost. This message is reinforced in Supergirl's avidly absorbed feminist literature, with the end result that Supergirl grows up despising supportive females, and determined never to become one.

The Tragedy of Supergirl

Supergirl's great tragedy is *not* that she believes in the legend that her father creates, for behind all the bluff she suffers chronic doubts as to her abilities and suffers an intense fear of failure. Her tragedy lies in the fact that she accepts the unattainable task of seeking to win her father's approval by attempting to fulfill his fantasies, and actually become amazing.

The hard truth, of course, is that very few normal people—and even fewer spoiled children—can ever hope to even begin to fulfill such expectations, for, by simple definition, truly amazing people, if they exist at all, really are extremely rare (which is why, of course, we have gods).

Supergirl has *some* talent, as most people have, and this with practice and effort she will be able to hone. Her major skill, however, and the one that carries her the farthest, is the knack of manipulating people, and especially men. Supergirl finds, very early in life, that Daddy is highly responsive to her girlish charm, and, soon enough, she is playing him like a violin. In later life, she turns this knack to advancing all kinds of deals, along with her own career.

The other side of Supergirl's persona, of course, is her anger. Some people would tell you she has a quick feline temper, while others might call her a bad-tempered bitch. Whatever description you care to put to it, she can be supercilious, haughty, sarcastic, vindictive, abrasive, and downright mean. And, although she most easily produces this side of her personality when crossed, she doesn't have to be genuinely crossed in order to do so.

Supergirl is highly sensitive to imagined slights, at which she will usually flare in a flash. She flies into these sudden furies for good reason, of course: she gets angry because she *is* angry. This anger is in response to her special predicament, the dilemma created for her by her father. On the one hand, he spoiled her, subtly raising her to be dependent upon him by remaining a *child*. On the other hand, he forced her to deny her underlying dependence in order to attempt to prove, both to him and to the world in general, that she is a truly outstanding *adult*.

Supergirl's response to the curse he has put upon her is anxiety, resentment, hostility, and bitter rage, in about that order. Of course, she tries to hide such feelings with what she likes to imagine is an Iacocca-type mask, but, every so often, to everybody's dismay, her true feelings burst from the cauldron scathingly into the open.

Supergirl deeply resents both her own dependence and the need to deny it. She hates continually having to prove that being something other than her true self somehow makes her "special." She particularly resents that winning this status entails her having to don the costume and mask of a stereotypical male business executive. These burdens, weighing upon her day and night, keep her tightly wound, and often subject her to insufferable stress. Little wonder, then, that ultimately she breaks down, just like the little girl that she is.

Supergirl's Education

Supergirl usually attends and graduates from as fine a private college as can be found to take her. Normally, she then goes on to graduate school, often picking up a master's in law, invariably at her parents' expense, of course. It is very common, too, after just a short stint in corporate life, to see Supergirl returning to college in pursuit of an M.B.A. Daddy will most likely encourage her in this endeavor, and gladly finance the operation, but, to be fair, Supergirl's own urge to

compete and win in "a man's world," together with the underlying desire to stay out of it for a couple more years, often
motivates this pursuit.

Supergirl's Career

Supergirl is much attracted by glamorous, traditionally
male organizations such as large stockbroking houses and investment banks. They, in turn, are ripe prey for Supergirls,
because, first, in our modern world such organizations need
to be seen to be nonsexist; and, second, because they *want* to
employ highly materialistically oriented (greedy) people with
strong manipulative skills.

So, Supergirl lands the job and has her chance to "make
it." And, to the surprise of no one, and the delight of many,
she meets with initial success, so much so that her boss, usually a youngish male with not too much experience of Supergirls, soon forms the opinion that she is "smart as hell, and
really can sell." In terms of intelligence, education, and manipulative skills, he is right, of course, and Supergirl thus
makes a great first impression with staff and clients, besides
giving a creditable performance that earns her quick promotion to a more senior selling role.

It is usually at about this point that Supergirl's capacity for
overall *judgment* turns out to be not quite as acute as everyone
had figured. She still sells to a lot of people and makes a lot
of deals, but now, strangely, quite a few things start to go
wrong. Some deals are somehow just not right, and in consequence other employees start getting burned. Alternatively,
when a potential client fails to accede to a particular deal or
sale, Supergirl is unable to control her underlying anger, gives
the demon free rein, then, when the client complains to her
boss, or takes his business elsewhere, simply tells bald lies

about her behavior or rationalizes that the client is one of those old-fashioned chauvinists who refuse to accept women on an equal footing.

Though some of her clients are left less than entirely satisfied, Supergirl does manage to talk her way out of the first few of these unfortunate situations, for she is after all a pretty good salesperson.

In fact, Supergirl is so strong a manipulator that she sometimes is able to produce a quite outstanding sales coup. A very real problem exists in reaching any accurate evaluation of her sales performance, however, for the fact of the matter is that her results are measured by a double standard, which, contrary to conventional wisdom, operates in her favor: thus, if she achieves the results of a good sales*man,* she is judged to be quite outstanding, and if she achieves the figures of an outstanding man, she is considered a genius.

On the basis of such results, plus the need to find and promote female executives, Supergirl is likely eventually to be plucked from the sales team, and, usually following much fanfare in at least the trade press, stuffed into a fairly senior management role.

Supergirl's Management Style

On the positive side, she does a great job of seeming to be a dyed-in-the-wool member of upper management. There is a constant stream of jargon-laden, buzz-word-bespattered, pontificating memos. She hires a male secretary, and *never* types herself ("I'm not falling into *that* trap," she says). She has her office refurbished, sometimes with antiques, other times with wildly modern artifacts. She buys even more Brooks Brothers suits, along with a pair of prepossessing executive spectacles. She encourages the press in their fervent desire to write feature articles detailing her meteoric rise and explaining her formula for success. And, of course, arriving by company limo, she entertains clients and prospects at famous restaurants in lavish style, if not always perfect taste.

When it comes to actually *doing* the job, however, when it comes to being a real executive—recruiting, supervising, leading and motivating a staff, solving hard problems, focusing a whole department, pulling everything and everyone together and producing ever greater profits—when it comes to these things that are the very essence of fine management, Supergirl makes a *very* poor showing. She fails because these tasks call for the clear, rational, adult head of a well-adjusted person capable of operating without too much in the way of supervision or reinforcement.

One of two things usually happens at this point: Supergirl either receives yet another "promotion," this time back into some kind of sales or public relations role where she can't do as much harm, or she is squeezed out.

It is then that Supergirl's entire psyche normally disintegrates, for the notion that she might actually have failed in a man's world is something she can admit to no one, least of all herself. Thus, if her fate is dismissal, she is likely to take the discharge in extremely bad grace, often to the point of suing the employer, claiming that she is some kind of victim, most predictably of sexist discrimination.

Supergirl usually works her way through a number of such employment situations and the pattern is nearly always identical: an outstanding interview, an attractive offer, good early sales or deal-making results, followed by a promotion to a position she cannot handle, and a flurried or frenzied departure. Those in the know seldom like to talk about what went wrong, sometimes because they don't quite know the real cause of the problem, occasionally for more delicate reasons.

Supergirl's Supermen

Supergirl almost inevitably experiences what her probable favorite magazine calls "relationship problems." There will be an unhappy first marriage, entered into either at or just after college, that fails for at least two reasons; the first being that Supergirl is a spoiled brat who has difficulty in establishing virtually any long-term relationship; the second being that she finds herself caught in the same double bind as the Queen Bee: most men *are* frightened of Supergirls, so that the kinds of fellows prepared to marry them are often wimps in search of mothers.

The thing to keep in mind is that Supergirl's relationship with her father, though unconsummated, is intrinsically sexual. Thus, later in life, like a female Don Giovanni—or perhaps the belle from Keats's poem "La Belle Dame sans Merci"—she is predestined to spend her days and nights falling in and out of love with men who simply cannot measure up to her idealized father.

This won't stop Supergirl from searching, of course, and so, quite apart from several marriages, she may be as sexually active as any red-blooded and maladjusted salesman. Her tendency to pursue unwise affairs is even further provoked by essentially infantile notions of what "making it" might actually include, and her confused concepts often lead to office affairs, sometimes with her clients, but more often with her father-figure superiors, including, on occasion, even the chief executive officer himself. This process is often euphemistically referred to in corporationland as "being mentored," a time-honored process that normally culminates in some highly sticky endings.

Supergirl's Endings

Supergirl's corporate career invariably concludes in one of two ways. In the first, best, and rarest, she meets, manipulates, and then marries an immensely powerful father-figure, such as one of her former chief executive officers or chairmen. Realizing that she is most unlikely ever to improve on this coupling, she then makes special efforts to hang onto her catch, to the point where the old lion, blinded by love, completely fails to comprehend Supergirl's shortcomings, and is flattered to have an attractive young wonderwoman for a wife. It is also likely that he may choose to indulge her lusts for status and power by promoting her to a high-profile position somewhere among his own business interests. Here, under his watchful eye, and with a capable staff to clean up after her, she may not do an awful lot of harm. Indeed, a *very* good public relations person might even be able to pass her off as some kind of genius, thus assuring Supergirl's career of a truly super climax.

The infinitely more likely ending, however, is that following a string of squeeze-outs, Supergirl finds herself unable to pull off any further hirings. Then, failing to meet a Mr. Right, or even a Mr. Close-Enough, she often turns to self-employment in some kind of sales role. Supergirl-in-mid-life is thus often to be found as the high-profile though only marginally successful principal of some kind of one-person agency, handling, say, advertising, fashion, personnel, real estate, or travel. She may also often be found selling and running assertiveness-training seminars, or unsuccessfully running for public office.

The key to this second ending is that Supergirl's final role satisfies some of her status needs, while compelling her either to modify the more unpleasant aspects of her personality or to go broke.

How to Manage a Supergirl

The best policy, quite obviously, is not to hire Supergirl at all. However, if you already have done so, the smart thing is to keep her very hard at work in a lower-echelon sales role, while resisting the blandishments of some young male executive who comes sidling up to you to say, "Hey, boss, this new girl we've hired down in the bond department is really aggressive and smart as hell. Maybe we could do something with her."

Don't even *think* about it.

SUPERGIRL IN BRIEF

BASIC TYPE:	Female reactive-dependent who seeks traditionally male role as some kind of big shot.
ROLE MODELS/HEROES:	Leona Helmsley, former real estate broker, currently president of Helmsley Hotels. Mary Cunningham, former corporate executive. Helen Gurley Brown, editor of *Cosmopolitan*.
FACADE:	Aggressive, tough, macho, highly confident.
COFFEE-TABLE LITERATURE:	*Wall Street Journal.* *Business Week.* *The Executive Female.* *Forbes* magazine.
FAVORITE SAYING:	"I'm a real tough manager."
APPARENT OBJECTIVE:	To achieve, to be the best.
REAL OBJECTIVES:	To fulfill scripting as Daddy's amazing protégée, by "making it in a man's world." To win status, celebrity, power.

UNDERLYING EMOTIONS:	Anxiety, resentment, hostility. Chronic fear of failure.
BEDSIDE READING:	*Having It All,* by Helen Gurley Brown. *Princess Daisy,* by Judith Krantz. *Self* magazine. *Cosmopolitan* magazine. *People* magazine.
MIGHT BENEFIT FROM READING:	*The Neurotic Personality of Our Time,* by Karen Horney. *The Cinderella Complex,* by Colette Dowling. *Smart Women, Foolish Choices,* by Cornell Cowan and Melvyn Kinder.
MANAGEMENT STYLE:	Alternately Miss Charm and angry autocrat.
STRENGTH:	Highly manipulative.
WEAKNESSES:	Inherently unsuited to the role to which she aspires. Emotionally weak. Highly dependent. Infantile judgment. Self-centered in the extreme. Not truly interested in accomplishment.

HOW TO SPOT: "Personality clash" with
former employer(s).
Prior history of litigation.
Pushy in dealing with your
secretary.
Consistently talks of her
"toughness."
Works her father into the
conversation, and tells
how much of her success
she owes to him.
Overprotected upbringing.
Seeks line-management role.
Carries press clippings
mentioning her toughness
or accomplishments.
Good appearance, expensive
clothes.
Seeks position calling for
"tough management."
Lives beyond means.
Embraces modern morality
following unhappy
marriage(s).

HOW TO MANAGE: Place only in structured role
calling for manipulative
skills.
Let go rather than promote.

14

Down in engineering . . .

LOCKHEED

The enemy of the market is not ideology but the engineer.
JOHN KENNETH GALBRAITH

LOCKHEED'S NAME, along with what is known as the "Lockheed Syndrome," springs from the plight of engineers working in the Seattle-based aerospace industry. In actuality, however, Lockheeds abound in virtually any geographically biased high-technology organization—as, for example, in the Silicon Valley–based computer industry.

Lockheed always had a strong scientific bent, something he probably inherited from a hard-driving, achievement-oriented father. As a kid, Lockheed owned a chemistry set, and almost certainly built either model planes or radios, perhaps both. At school he excelled, especially in the hard sciences. He didn't much care for languages or literature, couldn't be bothered to read novels, could make no sense of poetry, but loved every textbook he laid eyes on.

Lockheed is an introvert in at least two senses. First, he's cerebral and cold in his approach to life, much more interested in things than people, preferring to work alone and be alone. Second, he has the capacity to block out the world and to live entirely within the confines of his own head, either contemplating puzzles or solving them. Indeed, Lockheeds can be so intense that their parents sometimes fear they might be autistic.

Lockheed normally shuns sports in high school, preferring to devote himself to his studies, at which he normally excels, eventually winning a place at a fine technologically oriented college or institute. There, again, he immerses himself in learning, while particularly enjoying scientific experimentation and research.

Lockheed is recruited straight out of college, landing a good position with a major high-tech company, where he proceeds immediately to immerse himself in his work. He does a fine job and is quickly promoted to the most demanding projects.

The only diversion in Lockheed's life is his wife, whom he married because of proximity and the attraction of opposites. She was probably the girl next door, either at home or at college, and she is often as outgoing as Lockheed is withdrawn.

At Work with Lockheed

Lockheed is a workaholic, and, like all true workaholics, he both loves his job and suffers a deep unconscious desire to appease his superego. However, Lockheed is also an insecure fellow whose underlying unease provokes an intense perfectionism that compels him to forever seek perfect solutions, perfect products.

Lockheed becomes intoxicated with the joy of creating new things, but continually gets tied down in the minutiae created and intensified by his perfectionism. He works long hours, evenings, weekends. He would pitch a camp bed by his desk if he had to—indeed, many Lockheeds have been known to do just that.

One day, a recruiter calls to say that a high-paying client is prepared to offer Lockheed a much better job. Lockheed listens as the recruiter describes a wonderfully challenging role working within the industry leader's research team, where he would be managing his own design section.

The money is not all that much more than Lockheed is already earning, but he feels that the other attractions of the job—working with the best minds at the leading edge of the industry, in the most up-to-date facilities, using the latest and finest equipment, becoming a manager—are just too good to miss. By comparison, what he is doing now seems like making fire by rubbing two sticks together. The only catch is the relocation. He and Mrs. Lockheed will have to move to the town that houses this entire industry.

Lockheed's current employer makes an attractive counteroffer, but cannot induce Lockheed to stay, for the challenge of the new job means too much to him. Having to relocate is of little importance to Lockheed, for he seldom forms personal ties of any substance. When his wife points out that she will have to give up her friends, Lockheed simply shrugs his shoulders and mumbles something about the way the cookie crumbles.

Problems in Paradise

The Lockheeds pack up their kids (two, usually) and fly off to a neat, modern, ranch-style home, possessed of four bedrooms, two garages, two and a half bathrooms, a living room/dining room, a large family room, and a den or study. Mrs. Lockheed normally chooses clean-limbed functional furniture, including an Eames chair and matching ottoman, both of which she places in front of the television for Lockheed.

Lockheed goes immediately to work, where he quickly begins to labor harder and longer than ever. He likes the task, the environment, and the facilities. One thing he does not enjoy too much, however, is managing people; and, because Lockheed's style is that of the typical perfectionist, his subordinates seldom enjoy being managed by Lockheed, either.

Perfectionists may be described as people who take great pains and give them to others, and Lockheed is unlikely to be any exception to this rule. Normally, he is every bit as neurotically demanding of others as of himself. He involves himself in every detail of his subordinates' duties, and they can do little that he does not want improved or done over again. Indeed, managing (actually, doing) other people's work eventually takes up so much of Lockheed's time that he falls behind in his own work, and so doesn't have time for the creative tasks he most enjoys.

Lockheed's other problem has to do with making decisions. He devotes so much time and effort to searching for perfect answers that he suffers great difficulty in making any decision at all. Often, at the very moment when the facts of an issue seem to point one way, Lockheed somehow dredges up a new concern that balances everything out, thereby causing him to freeze in his tracks out of a morbid fear of doing the wrong thing. More and more of his response to challenges seems to be to try to worry the matter to death. He feels that if only he could give the problem enough thought, then he would be able to come up with the one absolutely right answer, the perfect solution that his brain tells him just has to be out there, somewhere. . . .

Soon enough, Lockheed is working a twelve- to sixteen-hour day, every day of the week, so that it is a very rare day that his young children get to see him. Lockheed also drives himself so hard that his temper becomes extremely quick to fray, both on the job and at home during the few hours he's not sleeping.

At Home

None of this inspires great joy in the heart of Mrs. Lockheed, of course. She has given up her friends and family to be with her husband, but he rarely comes home other than to sleep, and when he does is sour and short-tempered. She is often housebound with pre-school-age children during the day, thus all too often the only people she gets to meet are other similarly manacled women with kids of their own in tow. And, to compound her problems, the typical company town is a pretty dull place, affording little by way of diversion or employment for untrained women.

Thus, pretty soon, Mrs. Lockheed is so highly dissatisfied and frustrated that any discussion in the area of life-style turns quickly to fierce argument. The discussion is further intensified when Lockheed makes it very plain that he has absolutely no intention of leaving, period. Indeed, Lockheed usually lacks the empathy or sensitivity even to emotionally comprehend his wife's predicament, let alone to take any remedial action.

It is also worth noting that Lockheed is likely to be a poor father, perfectionistic and demanding of his children, angered when they fail to meet his highly unrealistic standards, and insensitive to, as well as intolerant of, any attempt on their part to make emotional contact with him.

The End for Lockheed

Not surprisingly, Lockheed's marriage normally collapses, the break often coming when his wife makes good on her threat either to pack up and go home to her folks, or find other male company. At this point, Lockheed simply devotes even more time and energy to his job.

Lockheed seldom gets to hold onto his managerial responsibilities for very long, however. He is too cold to lead and too perfectionistic to manage, and the strain of having to try to do so eventually impairs his own effectiveness as a creator or ace operator.

Lockheed's ultimate demise will be determined by the longevity of his creativity, which, contrary to popular belief, seldom improves with age, for, given a few notable exceptions, the creative process requires more energy than most men past their middle thirties are able or willing to give (which, of course, is why industries calling for outstanding creativity—such as advertising and computers—are traditionally arenas for comparatively youthful players).

Lockheed thus usually faces one of two endings. If he really can keep on producing, he lands the role of Boffin, one of those abstracted and impractical backroom types so much prized for the ability to come up with a really great idea. More frequently, however, he fails to shine, and his star simply fades. Although he is kept on the team, he is no longer regarded as a key member. Then, when the entire industry encounters a downturn, as such industries always do, Lockheed inevitably suddenly finds himself on the scrap heap.

How to Manage a Lockheed

In the high-tech corporate world, it's often highly tempting to attempt to make a manager out of Lockheed, but the move is normally a foregone failure. It's thus wisest to let Lockheed do what he does best, which is to work pretty much on his own.

As with most workaholics, he has to be saved from the kind of burnout that comes from lighting the candle at both ends and then attempting to maintain the glow over too long a period. Lockheed should therefore be forced—if need be—to take a three-week annual holiday. He should also be encouraged to live something akin to a normal life during the year.

A wise employer would probably also want to find a way to involve Mrs. Lockheed in some kind of company-organized social activities so that both Lockheeds have the chance to feel like members of the same team.

Stress counseling can also sometimes alert a Lockheed to the special problems engendered by his own personality type.

LOCKHEED IN BRIEF

BASIC TYPE:	Superstar of the engineering team.
ROLE MODELS/HEROES:	Steve Wozniak, co-founder of Apple Computers. Thomas Edison, inventor.
FACADE:	May be either deadly serious or highly childlike.
COFFEE-TABLE LITERATURE:	*Scientific American.* *Byte* magazine.
FAVORITE SAYINGS:	"I didn't quite hear you." "I'll try, but I've already got more on my plate than I can handle." "I need more hours in the day."
APPARENT OBJECTIVE:	To create a revolutionary product.
REAL OBJECTIVE:	To overcome feelings of insecurity by showing outstanding accomplishment and perfection.
UNDERLYING EMOTIONS:	Insecure around people, guilty if not working.
BEDSIDE READING:	Assorted science fiction.

MIGHT BENEFIT FROM READING:	*Gödel, Escher, Bach: An Eternal Golden Braid,* by Douglas R. Hofstadter. *On Becoming a Person,* by Carl Rogers.
MANAGEMENT STYLE:	Aloof autocrat, or, with any good luck, *primus inter pares* (first among equals).
STRENGTHS:	Energy, creativity, tunnel vision.
WEAKNESSES:	Naive. Impractical. Cool, lacking in empathy.
HOW TO SPOT:	Works in hi-tech area. Divorced, separated, or difficult marriage. Lives in company town, removed from familial origins, particularly of spouse. Introverted, dreamy-seeming. Hi-tech degree with outstanding grades. Interest in photography, or similar pseudo-scientific hobby. Perfectionistic parent(s). Out of work following fast rise based on technical bent.

	Confused as to what went wrong in his life.
HOW TO MANAGE:	Place in creatively oriented project and leave pretty much alone.
	Never promote above project leader.
	Make annual vacation compulsory.
	Encourage family-oriented spare-time interests.

15

From the country and making it big in the city . . .

RUSTY

Towered cities please us then, and the busy hum of men.
JOHN MILTON

The country only has charms for those not obliged to stay there.
ÉDOUARD MANET

RUSTY'S STORY is defined more or less equally by a not uncommon blend of environment and personality.

Rusty is the high achiever from the American hinterland— or maybe even a far-off country—who ultimately is rewarded with promotion to his company's corporate headquarters in New York, accompanied by some high-sounding title such as vice-president or international director.

Though a family man, Rusty is thrilled to relocate, for in his fantasies, Manhattan has always been the most fantastic of cities, a real-life land of Oz, a magic and enchanted Emerald City.

Rusty and his wife, Rustica, along with their two kids— probably a Red and a Sandy—all descend upon LaGuardia airport sometime during the summer break, so as to start the kids at school at the beginning of the semester. They typically catch their first joint view of the Big Apple early in the morning while arriving on a "red-eye" flight. As the plane wings down over the city, their heads flood with storybook images made brighter by adrenaline and jet lag.

When the Rustys leave the airport, however, they head for the hills rather than Manhattan, for the decision has been made, fatefully, to live outside the city, *way* outside. The rationale of this decision, apparently so wise at the time, is worthy of consideration, for it is crucial to an understanding of Rusty's personality, and of his central tragedy.

The Road to New Canaan

Rustica typically is hyperfearful of Manhattan. Newspapers and television have warned her, time and again, of the filth, the crime, the risk to her children, and, of course, the expense. Rusty, on the other hand, loves the notion of the "Big A" and all the glamorous images it conjures up. He knows, however, that maintaining a family residence in the city will be beyond his means, even on his newly elevated salary. Even if they took a small apartment, there'd still be the prohibitive cost of sending the kids to private schools, which you just *have* to do, as everybody knows, if you choose to live in Manhattan.

Rusty, however, doesn't want to live in the suburbs, feeling that he's had enough of Nowheresville: and, even more to the point, that the move to Manhattan, in conjunction with his rise in status and salary, calls for some kind of grand gesture.

Thus motivated, the Rustys hit upon what seems to be a great idea that will enable them to have the best of both worlds. Rusty will have to commute anyway, they reason, so, instead of getting off in the suburbs, he will simply stay on the train for an extra half hour. In other words, they will all live in the *country*, in a grand—but now affordable—rustic home. Rustica will thus be in a position to take in the Broadway matinees whenever she feels like it, while Rusty thrives upon a dynamic work environment plus the daily replenishment of a rural hideaway. Accordingly, after talking to a few people, the Rustys meet a wonderfully helpful real-estate agent who finds them a handsome house set on a tree-dotted two-acre plot abutting a gravel road.

Some years back, such havens were to be found at affordable prices in the then outer reaches of New Canaan, Connecticut, an hour or so from Manhattan. Nowadays, the astronomical costs of such Shangri-Las would push Rusty even farther into the New York hinterlands.

Rusty pays more than he expected to get what they really want; but, what the hell, he reasons, his appreciably higher income fully justifies a decent life-style—requires it, even.

The next expense, of course, is furnishing the place, but he's earning easily enough to get a hefty loan. Feeling that it might be important to be able to impress head-office visitors and houseguests, Rusty decides not to stint on the furniture, so they fill the house with really nice reproduction antiques.

Finally, of course, Rusty needs a second car for getting to and from the train. Rustica would chauffeur him, but the drive is just a little too long. Also, he'll be both leaving very early in the morning and often unsure of what time he'll be returning at night. At this point, Rusty typically decides to upgrade their old sedan to a new wagon for his wife, supplemented by a semiwreck to leave at the station without having to worry about its deterioration or theft.

With the props in place, Rusty now keenly contemplates the long-anticipated richer overall texture of life in the big time. The dynamism of his new work environment will daily push him to even greater achievements, yet he will be able to fully recharge his batteries during the evenings and weekends. And if, once in a while, his duties compel him to stay in town, well, that will be no hardship, for the Big Apple has compensating pleasures for people like Rusty, who of an evening have been known to slip into vagabond shoes.

Rusty's New Life

That first autumn season in Manhattan proves to be a lot of fun for Rusty. His day begins when he rises at six, showers, grabs coffee and toast, and drives to the station in time to catch the 6:55 into town. On the train, he reads the *Wall Street Journal* and the *New York Times*, relishing the time to devour both papers from cover to cover, which he feels will make him a better-informed person and thus an even more formidable executive.

Rusty gets into Grand Central at 8:03 and moves quickly to the teeming downtown subway, on which he swings from a strap for half an hour down to Wall Street. Finally, following a short walk, Rusty is at his desk sorting through the correspondence by a quarter of nine, and just rarin' to go.

Rusty's Executive Style

Rusty truly hurls himself into his work, and he is typically chosen for this drive, along with well-developed technical and people skills. He can be a little hostile, of course, but that's a normal characteristic of all "Type A's" like Rusty.

However, while Rusty's intellect is superior to the run-of-the-mill and his technical judgment mostly first-rate, he is also a dreamer, which is why, when it comes to relatively straightforward everyday issues, his undeniable creativity often leads him toward clever yet impractical solutions. This can and does get Rusty into trouble on the job from time to time, but for the most part the corporate structure keeps him on the rails.

Rusty's first Manhattan posting is normally to a staff role, the understanding being that this will enable him finally to prove his mettle among the heaviest hitters in the center of the universe. There, the first thing Rusty discovers is that business doesn't really seem to move all that much faster in Manhattan than in Nowheresville. Since head-office decisions have such wide ramifications, a good deal of time tends to be taken over them. Getting to the right decision, every time, becomes vitally important, so more care has to go into all the details. There's less margin for error than in the hinterland.

Rusty also finds himself spending much more time with people extremely keen to sell him their business services, and especially over expensive food and beverages. As is to be expected, Rusty enjoys being so courted, and happily throws himself into the infamous Manhattan lunch scene. One immediate consequence, however, is that he has to make up a lot of lost desk time, so that often he can't leave the office in time to catch his regular train. And, of course, when he does arrive home at around eight or nine in the evening, after having put in something akin to a fourteen-hour day, Rusty is usually too bushed even to talk to anyone, or even to watch television.

Rusty at Large

Soon enough—usually within about six months or so—Rusty decides that it's just not worth running himself into the ground to get home every single weekday evening. Instead, he will devote some of his commuting time to the job by working late at the office. Then he will stay in town for the night, either at the corporate apartment or in a room at the very nice midtown club the company paid for him to join.

Rusty discovers that this scenario offers quite a lot of fun. For openers, it's a pleasure not to have to worry about the train timetable, or about leaving the office by a fixed time. More time at the desk also makes him feel good as he catches up on his workload, and quickly makes new friends among kindred spirits, people like himself, individuals who like to work hard. Pretty soon he is also joining them in playing hard, too.

One way and another, it's not too long before Rusty finds himself, just for company, at first, eating dinner with one of those attractive, single, twenty-eight- to thirty-five-year-old women who have their own apartments right in Manhattan. And, of course, very soon they are not only making love but falling in love, or so they say. Rusty is, after all, attractive, fun, charming, intelligent, affluent, and male. To the new woman in his life the fact that he is also married is not immediately of great concern, for she knows from personal experience that the best men usually are.

Rusty's real love, of course, is for the notion of a Manhattan affair, *his* Manhattan affair. Now Rusty feels like a character in one of the many Manhattan film romances he has so much enjoyed and envied. Now it is *his* turn. He is enchanted by the fact that it is he, Rusty from Middle America—or anywhere in the world, for that matter—who is now enjoying sophisticated trysts and assignations, wining and dining a Manhattan-ite at a famous eatery. It is he, and not Jack Lemmon, who, after making love, lights a Lucky, and then lies and listens to Mancini's theme from *The Apartment* on all-night FM radio.

New-Canaan-itis

Rustica is by now trapped within a related but altogether different life-style. The first thing she discovers, after dropping the kids off at school and returning home, is how lonely it is in the "country." She had expected to be somewhat short of company for a little while as a result of leaving her family and former friends, of course. What she hadn't reckoned on was her almost total isolation. Her new home actually cuts her off from virtually everyone and everything. She cannot even *see* the neighbors coming and going. She can see nothing but the maple trees, weeping willows, and rhododendrons.

She finds, too, that their wonderful real-estate agent—who continues to be a friend, and often asks about the house— was an exception, for, far from being warm, the people of New Canaan tend to hold themselves somewhat aloof, and especially from newcomers. In fact, the people of New Canaan are not unlike many of Manhattan's permanent residents, who seldom care to invest time in newcomers who they feel will probably not be around for very long. Thus, at the supermarket or Little League practice, Rustica's efforts to bubble brightly receive polite but distinctly cool responses. Then winter comes, revealing that the house has a dampness and mildew problem, and also needs quite extensive work to keep out the arctic air. When the workmen leave, she finds herself as confined as a prisoner behind bars.

Rustica, of course, feels she would be able to cope with her predicament much better if only Rusty were around more, like he used to be, and particularly if he were more of the old bright self that he used to be. Now, when he does come home, he's always exhausted. Also, he's touchy and irritable. It's almost, she thinks to herself, as if he's resentful of having to come home at all. Speculating that Rusty might be having an affair, she hints to him of this possibility. Rusty is angrily defensive and they fall into a bitter fight, leaving a long-persisting sour aftertaste.

Rustica, unfortunately, is seldom a strong person, and thus she rarely possesses many internal resources upon which to draw. Consequently, she usually falls into her depression well before the advent of spring, at which point the doctor suggests she curtail her drinking and take Valium instead.

The thing to note, of course, is that Rustica's depression is an entirely normal response to—and part of—the syndrome in which both Rustica and her mate are trapped: the syndrome of "New-Canaan-itis," or, more completely, "I'll-take-the-train-in-from-New-Canaan-itis."

Pressures

By this stage, Rusty is under more pressure than at any time in his life. His commute, even two or three times a week, runs him ragged. His money difficulties, exacerbated by the cost of his affair, gnaw constantly at the lining of his stomach.

The affair, though he continues to enjoy it, frequently leaves him drained. He finds that being in love is every bit as tiring as working, and frequently even more so. It's not just all the new sexual demands, either, but the food, the wine, the shortage of sleep, the emotion, the lack of peace of mind—and, lately, the subtle but ever-increasing pressure to give up even more of his home life. There's also the pressure of having to hide what he's doing, both from Rustica and the folks at the office.

Finally, there's the pressure of actually having to get his job done, which Rusty finds he has also badly underestimated. He comes to see that, quite apart from dealing with Manhattan's distractions, his employer also requires Rusty to justify his salary, title, and relocation. He is expected to be able to produce at any time and all the time. And, lately, he just hasn't been up to it, which has caused questions to be raised very discreetly by his superiors. There are no secrets in corporations, of course, so everyone at the office knows all about Rusty's private life, and most mornings cannot help but notice the effects of it in his puffy face.

Rusty's Retreat

Rusty's reactions to the news of his relocation back to Nowheresville are mixed. To begin with, of course, he is angry, and decides to quit the company and stay in New York. To this end, he calls on a few headhunters. They, unfortunately, are not too impressed with his credentials. He seems not quite to have made the grade in Manhattan, they reason, never getting beyond a staff job, and now being returned to the outlands after less than two years. Thus reasoning, they turn down their thumbs. Rusty then badgers competitor companies into interviewing him, but they, in turn, merely turn up their noses, which he finds even more galling.

In the end, Rusty and Rustica decide to accept the relocation. They put their house on the market, usually selling it through the same farsighted and forever friendly real-estate agent. After deducting all costs, they show a small loss on the deal.

Once back home, Rusty usually quits the company, frequently to take a Wiseman role within a consulting firm that is impressed by and has a use for his "New York experience."

Inevitably, Rusty lands an assignment taking him back to New York for a few days, at which point he discovers that lightning really does not strike in the same place twice. The old flame will be out of town that week, she says, and somehow the whole place looks even grimier and more decayed than he remembered. With little in the way of influence or money to spend, the suppliers who once so eagerly courted him are not so keen to spend time with him, either. In the end, he is pleased to leave the city of his one-time dreams, hopefully for the last time, and to get back home to Rustica, the kids, and some "real people."

Sometime later, at a dinner party, Rusty responds to the question of a small-town friend who, bright-eyed, wants to know all about the Big A.

"Oh, it's a great place to visit," says Rusty. "But you wouldn't really want to live or work there."

How to Manage a Rusty

Corporate types immigrating to places like New York need to be counseled as to the special problems they may have to face. The Rustys should be instructed on the kinds of problems they will be likely to encounter, and the kinds of decisions they will have to make. Ideally, they should be introduced to others who have made the same or similar journeys.

Rustica, in particular, should be the recipient of generous counseling and assistance before, during, and after the move. More than anything else, she may need help in order to find a circle of friends, or even merely a sympathetic listener. Sometimes this will merely be a matter of getting the Rustys into a country club. Other times it may involve assigning a mentor's role to one of Rusty's superior officers, someone capable of just keeping a friendly eye upon Rusty, and making sure he doesn't go right off the rails. Easing Rusty and Rustica into such relationships, at least upon a first relocation, is an important part of the corporate personnel function.

RUSTY IN BRIEF

BASIC TYPE:	Corporate parvenu: naive new arrival in a major city.
ROLE-MODELS/HEROES:	Dan Rather, CBS news anchor. Tom Brokaw, NBC news anchor.
FACADE:	Charming, bright, fun-loving, somewhat urbane.
COFFEE-TABLE LITERATURE:	*Manhattan, Inc.* magazine. *New Yorker* magazine.
FAVORITE SAYINGS:	"People talk a lot of nonsense about New York." "If you can make it in your own hometown, you can make it anywhere."
APPARENT OBJECTIVE:	To make it big.
REAL OBJECTIVES:	To savor the hedonistic pleasures of the big city. To compensate for a sense of inferiority relative to his small-town origins.
UNDERLYING EMOTIONS:	Anxious, doubtful, feelings of inferiority.

THE TYPES

BEDSIDE READING:	*New York* magazine.
MIGHT BENEFIT FROM READING:	*The Wonderful Wizard of Oz,* by L. Frank Baum.
MANAGEMENT STYLE:	Impractical democrat.
STRENGTHS:	Energy, creativity, bright personality.
WEAKNESSES:	Naive. Impractical. Tender-minded. Negative in later years. Not truly a team player.
HOW TO SPOT:	Lives or has lived in a major city, but born in a small far-off town. Commutes more than two hours daily. Bright pleasure-oriented personality. Lives beyond income. Likes alcohol with lunch. Attended only modest schools or colleges. Status-conscious and possibly a name-dropper. Divorced, separated, or unhappily married. Shows signs of poor health. Often the son of working-class parents. Overestimates own capabilities.

HOW TO MANAGE: Counsel Rusty and Rustica
prior to relocation.
Provide an orientation
period following
relocation, and specific
emotional support groups
for Rustica.

16

Contemplating the way things look . . .

FLAK

*The businessman wants only two things said about his company—what he pays
his public relations people to say, and what he pays his advertising people to say.
He doesn't like anybody ever to look above, beyond, or over that.*
DON HEWITT, producer, "60 Minutes"

*I have found public relations to be the craft of arranging truths
so that people will like you.*
ALAN HARRINGTON

A FLAK is a corporate public relations officer who is part
advocate, part apologist, and part *Doonesbury.*

Flak serves as conduit between the company and its public.
His primary job is to defuse or cover up potentially embar-
rassing grievances, and to ensure that the company is perceived in the best light. The role calls for someone intelligent,
sensitive, good with words, practiced in the art of putting the
best gloss on things, and capable of dissembling, or, if need
be, even outright lying.

Flak also often liaises with the corporate advertising agency,
helping them to get a fix—sometimes clear, sometimes
murky—on the kind of corporate image being concocted,
promoted, or preserved. The distinction between a corporate

Flak and a journalistic hack might not seem too great, but in actuality it is profound: the hack is usually free to tell the truth, whereas the Flak is paid to hide it.

Flak's Early Years

Flak is normally a thoughtful, facile, moderately bookish kid, who helped edit the school magazine and later wrote the college sports pages. Literature isn't his long suit, but he may well turn out some blank verse or the odd short story or two.

Flak's middle-class mother usually encourages her son's sensitivity and talent as a communicator. Generally he attends a college with a very modest reputation, studying things like literature, history, and politics, and getting average grades.

He likes to air his opinions, and is quite likely to have dee-jayed on the college radio station. He would also probably have joined the liberal club, grown his hair to his shoulders, and made the peace sign to his friends.

Flak courts conservative disdain, but is deeply wounded when liberal peers call him a lightweight, for his whole being is wrapped up in what he calls his "intellectual integrity," along with his finer feelings, and the wish to be seen to have done something worthwhile, or at least a little arty.

Into the Workforce

Flak is likely to have dreamed of becoming a part of some big movement and going a long way in it. His first job out of college is thus often in small-time politics, maybe working as volunteer for the local state senator. Here Flak learns about fund-raising and publicity, about compromise and flattery, about peddling influence and getting out a good press release.

In particular, he learns how to deal with and befriend the members of the local press.

By this point in his career, Flak is likely to be driving a small, previously owned European car, and to be wearing bow ties, pastel shirts, natural-shouldered tweed jackets, flannel trousers, and neat black loafers. It is around this time, too, that Flack becomes struck with the realization that politicians lack purity of motive, and that they also do not pay their professional helpers enough money.

Flak's Mate

Flak usually settles into a romantic relationship with a small, sweet, dependent female who might have worked for a while as assistant to the editor of a literary magazine. They would normally marry upon the advent of her pregnancy, at which time they would probably also decide to purchase and renovate a small apartment or a tiny house in a working-class but becoming-fashionable inner-city suburb. They would also feel that the time had come for Flak to cash in on his talent and experience, and seek a secure job paying a really decent salary.

A Career in Advertising

A career in advertising or public relations now appears to be the natural move for Flak, for it seems obvious that his intelligence and charm will command a pretty good income in such arenas. He vows, however, to "make it" without ever selling out his liberal principles: Flak's not going to prostitute himself for anyone, he says.

After looking at a few of the big agencies, Flak discovers that they really do put a premium on talent. You have to be able to write copy that actually sells things, which proves a lot harder than Flack had imagined. Fortunately, however, Flak hits upon an opening in the customer end of the business and becomes an account executive. This is fun for a while, but he soon discovers, to his horror and chagrin, that pleasing the client somehow always seems to call for the dirtying of one's nose in the end. As Flak's principles do not permit this luxury, he eventually falls into strong conflict with his employer, provoking his sudden departure from the firm.

Into the Real World

At this point, Flak normally seeks a position outside of the advertising profession, in what he calls "The Real World." Sure, he could have gone to another agency, but he somehow just didn't feel up to being on the wrong side of the table again. Better to be the client. Let them kiss *his* ass for a change.

Flak usually gravitates to a so-called glamor industry where, largely on account of his political experience and smooth manner, he may well land a position serving an illustrious if somewhat quirky and egomaniacal captain of industry. At first, Flak deals principally with the firm's ad agency, listening carefully to their suggestions, then later winning credit with his boss by passing the best ideas off as his own.

Eventually, this works out so well that Flak is made director of public relations. Now he sits in with the action committees, and sometimes even advises the chief privately on matters such as image-building and community relations. Flak also does a good job of keeping his chief's alcohol problem out of the press. Indeed, Flak proves to be at his best when operating in such sophisticated areas, all the way from arranging consulting assignments for politicians' wives, to providing clients with get-togethers where they are serviced by wonderfully discreet and attractive escorts.

Flak's conscience sometimes pricks him a little, but he rationalizes that his cause is just: the boss might have big warts, but he is still a great man. And, what the hell, isn't Flak helping to assure the tenure of literally thousands of employees, people as good and decent as he himself?

Flak's Management Style

Flak's a dabbler, who can play with ideas, write a readable paragraph or two, and effectively tie up a lot of loose ends. Unfortunately, however, he's not a manager. Though he may sometimes be put in charge of a small public relations department, this invariably proves to be a mistake, for Flak is no leader of men and never will be. A perfectionist, he also involves himself in too many details, and often asks for completed work to be redone. Finally, there is usually a reshuffling of duties, at which point Flak finds himself working on his own again, but sharing dotted-line responsibility with the advertising department.

Flak's Endings

Flak would normally sell his first home for a handy profit, then move a little farther out of town "for the sake of the kids." The new home might be a small, very affordable cottage that the Flaks would again renovate very tastefully, thereby keeping their overhead within reason, so as to prepare themselves for a rainy spell in their lives.

A congenital worrier, Flak frets about his job security, but masks this concern with remarks such as "I'm really proud of what I've done, and what I can do for my company"; and "The last guy they ever fire is the PR man."

In actuality, however, Flak is always close to the firing line, for the fruits of his labor are murky and unquantifiable, causing his name to quickly surface whenever the subject of unnecessary overhead is raised.

If fired, Flak would almost certainly seek the same kind of work—and encounter the same set of problems—in some other enterprise, for he normally lacks the drive, confidence, or talent to attempt anything else. Thus, one way and another, Flak lives on to develop a strong resentment of the free enterprise system, which he will tell you rewards the wrong kind of people for doing the wrong kinds of things. Flak usually manages to hide these feelings when in the presence of his job superiors, but is not always so politic in the company of subordinates, especially after a libation or two.

Flak also talks about writing a novel, but never gets around to it. Instead, to take his mind off his problems, he often gets serious about jogging, or pumping himself up on bodybuilding equipment in a health club.

The great success of Flak's life would probably be to put a son through college, then have him become a reporter for a good newspaper, from where he could look down upon the old man.

How to Manage a Flak

Flak's deepest emotional needs are for economic security, and a sense of contributing to a worthwhile cause. Thus, in managing him, it is well to point out that you and your company are in business principally to serve the public, that you take this responsibility very seriously indeed, and that, as long as he does a sound workmanlike job, his tenure will be secure.

Since Flak is seldom the creative person he seems, you should be prepared to come up with ideas of your own and have him work on them, rather than to expect him to initiate ideas. He can be relied upon to do a reasonably good job of getting out numerous routine press releases, and so on, which, let's be honest about it, tends to be the more important aspect of his role.

Don't ever be tempted to set up a department under Flak, for this will hamper rather than help him. Don't, either, have an outside agency or "idea person" reporting directly to him. Flak should always be a point of liaison, rather than an arbiter of creative worth.

If he ever says he wants to leave your employ, then by all means help him to find a more satisfying role somewhere else.

FLAK IN BRIEF

BASIC TYPE:	Idealistic corporate public relations officer.
ROLE MODELS/HEROES:	Pierre Salinger, press secretary to John Kennedy. Ron Ziegler, press secretary to Richard Nixon. Jody Powell, press secretary to Jimmy Carter. Dick Cavett, talk show host.
FACADE:	Serious, intelligent go-getter with integrity.
COFFEE-TABLE LITERATURE:	*Atlantic Monthly.*
FAVORITE SAYING:	"The last person they ever fire is the PR man."
APPARENT OBJECTIVE:	Early life: to be part of a great cause.
REAL OBJECTIVE:	Mid-life on: economic security; to be nurtured and cared for.
UNDERLYING EMOTIONS:	Feelings of helplessness, frustration, resentment.
BEDSIDE READING:	*Mother Jones.* *Doonesbury* anthology.
MIGHT BENEFIT FROM READING:	*How to Be Your Own Best Friend,* by Mildred Newman and Bernard Berkowitz.

MANAGEMENT STYLE:	Perfectionistic anarchist.
STRENGTHS:	Strong achievement needs. Sound interpersonal skills. Pliable. Personable.
WEAKNESSES:	Only moderate intellectual skills. Highly unrealistic, naive. Greatly overvalues his own and the corporation's contribution to society.
HOW TO SPOT:	Currently in charge of agency relations or publicity for corporate employer. Earns lowest-level management-scale salary. Formerly with advertising or public relations firm. Proud of his intellect. Says he is more than "just a corporate type." Speaks of his integrity. Studied literature at second-tier college. Interested in liberal politics. Didn't go to Vietnam. Well-spoken, charming, earnest, somewhat boyish. Dresses with refined sense. Owns modest European car.

Married to pretty, clinging wife who wishes he earned more.

Lives in blue-collar inner-city neighborhood that he hopes will "catch on."

Talks about writing a serious novel.

Wine buff.

HOW TO MANAGE: Feed with ideas.

Focus underlying altruistic needs.

Don't promote to management.

Monitor tendencies to unrealism.

17

Spending less time at the office . . .

FLANNELMAN

*How did I get here? Somebody pushed me. Somebody must have touched
his hands to the controls and set me off in this direction,
for I would not have picked this way for the world.*
JOSEPH HELLER

FLANNELMAN'S well-cut suit continues to bespeak
his commitment to corporate life. The furrows in his brow tell
another story, however: they say that his costume has lately
become too tight to accommodate his heart.

A Flannelman is a person who was raised to be a great executive, dreamed of becoming one, and worked very hard to
try to make that dream come true, but, unfortunately, just
didn't have the pizzazz, the bounce, the bite, the sting, the
chutzpah to make it to the top. Worse yet, he doesn't find all
this out until mid-life, at which point, after a bad dose of the
famous blues, he suddenly realizes that the game wasn't worth
the candle anyway. Now, Flannelman resolves to change, to
ease up, to make the time to "enjoy life's real pleasures before
it's too late."

Regrettably, however, he now discovers, somewhat to his
dismay, that giving up the game is not quite that easy, for, despite his new "maturity," a gnawing urge to fulfill those long-

held dreams continues to smolder somewhere in his stomach. He denies this publicly, of course, but he silently resents the younger executives who pass him in the corridors, and who now sometimes quite openly try to pass right over him as they attempt to climb the notoriously greasy corporate pole.

Flannelman puffs a pipe and plays at being corporate Wiseman, but by now he is decidedly ambivalent about the corporation that took so much of his life for so little return. Slowly, his idealism turns to out-and-out cynicism, that last refuge of the frustrated idealist.

The Making of Flannelman

Flannelman is often the middle child of a successful business executive, raised on traditional values in a middle-class home. He is taught that "success" is an honorable thing for which to strive, and told that the way to make it to the top is to be loyal, decent, and industrious.

Flannelman attends a good if not a great college, where he labors assiduously and in return gets fairly decent grades. He especially enjoys the liberal arts, and is inclined to an appreciation of things aesthetic. Since he is programmed to prize business success, however, he pursues an M.B.A. rather than the master's in history that held more appeal for him.

Flannelman sees the economic sense in Adam Smith, and he very much likes the idea of corporate life, regarding it as an advanced system in which a group of thoroughly worthwhile people give their best for the good of the team, the town, the flag, the world, and themselves. He sees his M.B.A. as his membership card to this club, as something akin to a "license to practice," with the subject being business rather than medicine or law. At business school, he thoroughly enjoyed the semester on ethics, and still very much likes to get into deep discussions on the subject—in the company of his intellectual peers, of course.

Flannelman's Family

Flannelman normally marries in his middle twenties, to the kind of girl one might want to take home to a thoroughly decent mother. Indeed, Flannelman's wife often acts and looks just like mother, being feminine, supportive, caring, somewhat apprehensive, and given to trim pastel blouses and tweed skirts. The Flannelmans most likely met in college, where she was probably studying art. She generally shares Flannelman's devotion to family, business, and community. She seldom has a paying job, but often works as a charity volunteer, probably for the Episcopal church.

The Flannelmans usually live in a nice house in a fine suburb, and are likely to own a small European car, a ranch-style station wagon, a two-car garage, a swimming pool, a well-groomed lawn, and a nice "library" filled with Book-of-the-Month Club Selections that they say they will definitely get around to reading someday, after the kids leave home.

The Flannelmans usually have a couple of children, who attend the very acceptable local school, where they get good if not spectacular grades, and then go on to attend second-tier private colleges with names like Briar Manse. The fees are a burden to the Flannelmans, but they tighten their belts and murmur through pursed lips that it's going to be money well spent.

Flannelman's Career

Flannelman starts out wanting to be a high achiever within an established corporate setting, usually joining a large corporation engaged in "something worthwhile," such as developing and bringing pharmaceuticals to mankind. He sets his sights on "running his own show" as president of a small-to-medium-sized division.

Flannelman's bright eyes, steadfast manner, and down-to-earth common sense impress his superiors, who fairly quickly put him onto the fast track via exposure to several departments to get a quick feel for the whole organization. Later, he may be assigned to work at the elbow of one of the senior line managers. Flannelman impresses everyone: easygoing and intelligent, he puts in long hours, works hard, and obviously has a great future. In his second-to-last promotion, he becomes "right hand" to Bluster Rough, the hard-driving manager of production.

Flannelman's contemplative style has a happy effect on Bluster's impulsive tendencies. Bluster doesn't always agree with Flannelman, but he comes to respect and increasingly rely upon Flannelman's well-reasoned advice. Bluster particularly encourages Flannelman to analyze trouble spots and put out fires. Flannelman does such a good job of this under Bluster's wing that he is eventually singled out for promotion to an important line-management position.

The promotion goes straight to Flannelman's stomach, however. With no pragmatic, experienced Bluster Rough in the wings to hold his hand if needed, Flannelman's decision-making apparatus breaks down. Nothing is easy anymore, and now Flannelman stews over even the simplest decisions. He tries to please everyone and thereby pleases no one. His subordinates sense his uncertainty, and his anxiety proves contagious. Morale falters, and Flannelman's inability to make decisions adversely affects the entire assembly line. Production halts pending Flannelman's pondering as to which model should be in the works for next autumn.

After a great deal of research, analysis, and heartache, Flannelman is forced to come to a decision. The next day, he reverses himself, then, three days later, reverses himself again.

The board hauls Flannelman back to the head office and makes him a senior vice-president in charge of nothing, but, as a sop, reporting directly to the chief executive officer. It's as good a job as Flannelman could ever have hoped for under the circumstances. He keeps his quite handsome salary, he retains a certain status, he continues to mix with nice people in trade associations and the like, he entertains some important customers, and he has plenty of time to contemplate the subtleties of corporate life.

How to Manage a Flannelman

Flannelmen tend to be sensitive and lonely people, frequently believing that they alone possess genuine understanding of what the world is all about. Thus, it is very important to let a Flannelman see that you share his finer feelings, that you fully appreciate his profound perceptions of the world and its ways.

Flannelmen often respond to psychotherapy, and they are among the few who might just thank you for steering them in that direction.

You might also give some thought to making Flannelman your in-house Wiseman, perhaps by way of either the human resources or public relations departments. Such a move could be on an informal basis. The important thing is for Flannelman to be able to feel that his new-found wisdom is at least getting a little air.

FLANNELMAN IN BRIEF

BASIC TYPE:	Failed organization man.
ROLE MODELS/HEROES:	Adlai Stevenson, former candidate for president of the United States. George Bush, vice-president of the United States.
FACADE:	Dedicated, loyal, hardworking, a "company man."
COFFEE-TABLE LITERATURE:	*The Lonely Crowd,* by David Riesman. *The Affluent Society,* by John Kenneth Galbraith.
FAVORITE SAYINGS:	"Can we really do that, ethically?" "My professor always used to say . . ."
APPARENT OBJECTIVE:	Originally to become a respected executive.
REAL OBJECTIVE:	To survive with a little dignity.
UNDERLYING EMOTIONS:	Feelings of inferiority, extreme frustration with the company, internalized anger.

BEDSIDE READING: Collected columns of William Buckley.

MIGHT BENEFIT FROM READING: *The Arrangement*, by Elia Kazan.
The Seasons of a Man's Life, by Daniel Levinson.

MANAGEMENT STYLE: Impotent democrat.

STRENGTHS: Strong achievement needs.
Hardworking.
Sound interpersonal skills

WEAKNESSES: Not a truly strong person.
Somewhat unimaginative.
Basically dependent.
Not a leader.

HOW TO SPOT: From the middle class, or sometimes the so-called American "upper" class (meaning "old-monied" class).
Soundly educated.
Usually possesses business degree.
Wears gray flannel suit or equivalent.
Stable job history.
Lives with pleasing family in attractive suburban home.
Works in prestigious corporation.

17. FLANNELMAN

HOW TO MANAGE: Relieve of line-status role.
Award status.
Promote to formal company
    Wiseman.
Include, where possible, in
    key discussions.

18

Not entirely comfortable on the team . . .

TOKEN

*If you want to make beautiful music
you must play the black and the white notes together.*
RICHARD NIXON

A TOKEN EMPLOYEE is by definition a person who holds a job by virtue of his or her race, color, sex, or creed. An employer would normally award such a job so as to comply with United States antidiscriminatory laws calling for the employment and subsequent promotion of minority candidates. Such token employees are thus usually black, Hispanic, or female, or any combination of the three.

Other notable types of token include the outsider who gains membership to an ingroup, such as, say, the Jewish employee in the predominantly Wasp firm. Then there's the insider who works for a traditionally outsiders' group, such as the Wasp who joins the predominantly Jewish firm.

Let's look a little more closely at these people.

Amber—The Darker Token

The fact of Amber's pigmentation is actually quite vital, for it means that he (or, quite often, she, but for smoother syntax we'll stick to one sex) is often going to be reacted to—and usually prejudged—from, quite literally, the very moment he becomes visible. Tokens who happen to share the same skin color as the ingroup are not immediately recognizable as aliens, and thus are often free to attempt to pass themselves off as bona fide members of that group.

One of Amber's greatest strengths, then, has to be his ability to overcome the mixed reactions caused by the fact of his coloring, and then to go on and gain acceptance within a potentially hostile group, for without this ability, Amber would never win or hold onto the job.

Amber's ability to win acceptance in the face of a mixed first showing springs from a subset of factors, usually including:

The credentials of a fine college. Whatever his intellectual skills may be, Amber can usually point to fine academic credentials, usually including a master's degree, often even a doctorate. These qualifications have generally been bestowed by a college held in special esteem by the employer.

Earning such qualifications may sound like a tall order. In fact, such educational opportunities can be more readily available to reasonably intelligent potential Tokens than to members of former elites, for modern colleges have quotas of their own that must be filled with minority students.

Physical attractiveness. Physical attractiveness is a quality often shared by successful people, and this normally holds true for Amber. Any physical advantage is also typically enhanced by sound dress and grooming skills, including, in particular, the kind of wardrobe favored by Amber's employer peer group. Thus, as an example, in a banking environment,

Amber will look like the quintessential Wall Street banker, rather than, say, a member of the Black Panthers.

A passive personality. Despite his education and attainments, Amber is normally a very passive, obedient, and strictly nonthreatening personality, for otherwise he would almost certainly never have been employed, or, having been employed, would never have survived. People get the feeling that Amber is always happy to do as instructed, and, indeed, this is usually true. Ambers usually are pleased to follow orders, for that was how they won their scholarships, their degrees, and their place in the alien world. Sure, they have the capacity to be charming, too, but this is usually very much a secondary aspect of their nature.

Identification with the employer. Amber's appearance and presentation are further complemented by behavior indicating a sophisticated appreciation and sympathy for the employer's value system and predicament vis-à-vis minority candidates. Amber thus feels free to tell jokes against his own race, indeed, often even to the point of making himself the butt of such stories. Amber's real aim here, however, is to subtly ingratiate himself with the employer group by distancing himself from his origins. Amber is also telling his employer that he is not a troublemaker or boat-rocker, and can be trusted to uphold the values of the group, even against his own people.

Gold—The Brighter Token

Gold takes his name from the story of a Jew who rises to serve the United States president in the White House, in Joseph Heller's novel *Good as Gold.*

For our purposes, Gold is the person of humble ethnic origins who joins a ruling "upper" and alien class, perhaps the Jew made partner in a "white shoe" or Wasp firm.

Unlike Amber, however, Gold is not initially disadvantaged by the "wrong" skin pigmentation, a fact that Gold capitalizes upon by honing his appearance until he is virtually indistinguishable from senior members of the firm. Gold also usually goes to great pains to think and behave like White-shoe, sometimes to the point of Anglicizing his family name, thereby, he hopes, removing the final clue to his origins. Also, he takes great care, in furnishing his office, to include photos of himself out horseback-riding, or walking the golden retriever with the children, off to attend a white-shoe school.

Mrs. Gold is highly likely to be—and very much seen to be—an out and out Wasp. Gold is likely to have fallen head over heels in love with her pert nose and country club manners, and the doors such things can open. However, Mrs. Gold's real beauty lies in the air of horsey legitimacy she brings to Gold's pretensions. She, clearly, is one of *them*—so Gold must now be one of them, too. Some people are likely to be as ambivalent toward the coupling as the former Kennedy admirer who, hearing of Jacqueline Kennedy's betrothal to Aristotle Onassis, is reported to have remarked, "She's gone from a Greek god to a goddamn Greek." For the most part, however, such remarks will seldom reach Gold's ears, and, indeed, the Golds will likely be a welcome duo at most Wasp social occasions.

It should be stressed, however, that Gold's concern with appearances seldom comes at any cost to his on-the-job performance. Indeed, he is likely to be possessed of an outstanding intellect, his natural intelligence having been honed to a sharp edge by the voice of his superego, his burning ambition, and a thorough education marked by outstanding grades.

Gold is usually highly attuned to subtlety and nuance, and

naturally adept at befriending his colleagues, and especially his superiors. He is also likely to be a first-class salesperson, of course.

Gold is normally very grateful to win White-shoe's acceptance in the form of a partnership, or whatever. Indeed, Gold may well go so far as to regard his ascension to partner status as the penultimate achievement of his life—the ultimate being to have his son do the same.

In fact, however, White-shoe deserves little in the way of gratitude, for he usually offers Gold the partnership only at such time as Gold has turned in an extraordinary performance, at which point White-shoe's motives are likely to be far more financial than collegial.

Blue—The Flawed Token

Blue takes his name from the color of his blood. He is the member of a supposedly superior caste group who is recruited to work for a supposedly inferior caste group, perhaps the white Anglo-Saxon Protestant who works for the otherwise all-Jewish firm.

Blues are often fatally flawed by the "poison ivy syndrome," a malaise affecting many of the children of those already very well-to-do American parents so hopelessly addicted to the pursuit and prizing of outstanding success in banking or finance. A Blue about to be so stricken is indulged and spoiled, prior to being sent off—assuming he has the credentials to get in—to a great American college, usually one of the big three, Harvard, Yale, or Princeton. If he doesn't have the moxie, the family, if rich enough, will often purchase this vital honor for him by endowing a chair or giving a library.

Blue's grades tend to be very ordinary, but he invariably graduates nonetheless. Then, by virtue of his connections, familial and collegial, he lands a good job in a fine old firm. Everyone expects him to become a great success, like the Old Man or Uncle Bartholomew, but, tragically, poor old Blue just can't hack it. Stunted by his upbringing, and poisoned by his Ivy League college, the fellow just cannot find any way to stand on his own emotional feet.

Connections carry the poisoned Blue just so far, but, by about age 40, he is frequently a very sour and sometimes even a downright suicidal character. And yet, although so deeply frustrated by his own impotence, he still has no real inkling as to what went so terribly wrong. Often he will eventually drop out, sometimes opting to "serve mankind," perhaps as a missionary or a schoolteacher.

Alternatively, Blue is recruited—and prized—by a supposedly inferior caste group, precisely because his origins and values are opposite to those of his employer. Blue is encouraged to display the appurtenances and uniform of his origins: to look, sound, and behave like a Wasp (or whatever). If the name on his engraved business card can be embellished by a III, IV, or V, then so much the better.

Blue is seldom bothered by the notion or the act of selling his breeding and contacts. His externalized justification is usually that he has to earn a living, but, in reality, he often quite enjoys the situation in that his employer normally treats him with a great deal of respect, certainly far more than the members of Blue's own clan. Also, he is well paid but not expected to work particularly hard, nor to sully himself with too much unseemly detail. His job is simply to be "on the team" (and especially the letterhead), and to allow his friends and contacts to be drawn into suitable business opportunities.

The Imposter Syndrome and the Role of the Token

Though some of them might deny it, most Tokens tend to at least partially recognize that they are impostors, believing deep in their hearts that they are not authentically successful people. And, indeed, it is almost impossible for Tokens to feel otherwise, for their sense of identity involves a denial of their innermost selves: they are both alienated from their origins, and dependent for any future success upon continuing the role and game in which they have been cast.

On a more positive note, however, we can say that Tokens have made a great contribution to society by becoming, at the very least, legitimate role models for those sharing similar cultural backgrounds.

The introduction of hitherto "alien" people into the workforce has also changed some attitudes and prejudices, making it much more possible for capable, well-adjusted people of disparate backgrounds to gain legitimate acceptance and acclaim in corporate life.

All in all, then, Tokens might have made a greater contribution than they themselves as individuals might ever fully realize.

TOKEN IN BRIEF

BASIC TYPE:	Executive appointed by virtue of minority status, or opposing cultural heritage.
ROLE MODELS/HEROES:	Arthur Ashe, captain of U.S. tennis team. Zbigniew Brzezinski, adviser to Jimmy Carter. T. E. Lawrence ("Lawrence of Arabia").
FACADE:	Competent, reliable, secure.
COFFEE-TABLE LITERATURE:	*Amber: Town and Country* magazine. *Gold: Up the Organization,* by Robert Townsend. *Blue: Social Register.*
FAVORITE SAYINGS:	"Have you heard the one about the black who . . ." "At the country club my wife and I . . ." "I know the family very well, in fact . . ."
APPARENT OBJECTIVE:	*Amber:* To do a good job and survive. *Gold:* To do an outstanding job and advance. *Blue:* To do whatever is asked.

REAL OBJECTIVE:

Amber: To do a good job and escape the past.
Gold: To win acclaim for an outstanding job, thereby escaping pervasive feelings of ethnic inferiority.
Blue: To maintain an inflated life-style.

UNDERLYING EMOTIONS:

Feelings of inadequacy, and of being an impostor.

BEDSIDE READING:

Amber: The Kennedys, by Peter Collier.
Gold: Good as Gold, by Joseph Heller.
Blue: Social Register.

MIGHT BENEFIT FROM READING:

The Impostor Phenomenon, by Dr. Pauline Clance.

MANAGEMENT STYLE:

Amber: Nonthreatening democrat.
Blue: Imperious loner.
Gold: Machiavellian democrat.

STRENGTHS:

Sound education, good interpersonal skills, wants to be on the team.

WEAKNESSES:

Chronic fear of failure. Often unable to function in unstructured role.

18. TOKEN

HOW TO SPOT: Member of minority on the
job.
Well-presented.
Attractive, personable.
Role-aware.
Careful to ingratiate self.
Degree(s) from prestigious
institution.
Nonthreatening.
Suffers unconscious
compulsion to draw
attention to fact of
minority status.

HOW TO MANAGE: *Amber:* Structure role,
nurture, build esteem.
Gold: Set challenges, offer
status as reward.
Blue: Structure role *very*
closely, permit little use of
initiative.

19

Attempting to get her act together . . .

DILLY

Dilettantism, as we all know, is the nonserious dabbling within a presumably serious field by persons who are ill-equipped—and actually do not even want— to meet even the minimum standards of that field, or study, or practice.
BEN SHAHN

DILLY is a housewife in a business suit. She is a dilettante, a breathless amateur in love with the notion of being seen to be a successful professional.

Dilly is often the only or eldest child of all-female siblings. Raised to believe that she just *is* smart and special—and thoroughly spoiled in the process—Dilly is denied contact with reality, and thus remains unrealistic and frustrated for the rest of her life. She feels that she should, by right, be able to enjoy the status and rewards of an "executive position," which, in her mind, means filling a prestigious and traditionally male role somewhere in corporationland.

Usually well educated, her parents probably having paid for her to complete at least one degree, and believing she is "talented"—as, indeed, many dilettantes are to some extent— Dilly feels that handling such a job ought to be pretty much a pushover for her.

To friends and recent acquaintances, Dilly is both person-

228

able and apparently carefree. She takes trouble with her grooming and thus "presents" very well. Behind this facade, however, she is self-centered, ambivalent, and deeply un-happy.

Wanting to succeed in a man's world, and believing that she can make it on her talent, Dilly is not an aggressive feminist. She is, however, given to championing causes, and especially those offering the opportunity to serve on a committee as spokesperson, president, or, ideally, both. Preferring her causes to be prestigious, she is attracted to worthy institutions in need of saving, such as museums and opera companies. Unfortunately, such charitable affiliations seldom last long, for Dilly has the unhappy knack both of making a mess of the task itself and of rubbing the other people involved the wrong way, and especially the loyal female volunteers, whom she tends to regard as "mere housewives." Soon enough, Dilly is tired of playing these "petty games," and, following much ear-nest talk with her loved ones, decides to exploit her talent in the "real world."

At this point, it is quite possible that Dilly's husband will support her while she acquires a mid-life post graduate qual-ification, motivated by her feeling that if she could show some sort of technical certificate, then an employer would be almost duty-bound to give her a chance.

In fact, the odds on Dilly landing a good job as a token female are fairly high, given the number of management po-sitions that nowadays must by law be offered to women.

In the first instance, Dilly will probably be very pleased to be offered some kind of disguised sales role, perhaps as an "investment adviser" or "stockbroker." This kind of job is initially attractive to Dilly because it offers the status of a "professional" male, along with the opportunity to earn "big bucks." Dilly soon finds, however, that even stockbrokers have to *produce:* that they have to establish their own clientele, then go on to service it, then rebuild it, then service it again, then rebuild and service it all over again, and again, *ad nauseam.*

This is definitely not what Dilly had anticipated, and she finds that she has underestimated both the amount of work involved and the degree of skill required to maintain even a holding position in a tankful of professional sharks. She finds, too, that the serious investor is unforgiving of the "little boo-boos" that characterize her performance under pressure. Suddenly, the world is peopled with individuals who seem to be downright *unkind.* Unlike Daddy, or her old friends Buffy and Wendy and Freddie and Charles, these nasty new people merely become increasingly annoyed the more she flashes her winningly girlish smile. Daddy used to love it, and Hubby quite likes it, but it cuts no ice with the clients. Sometimes they even get *really* angry with her. All they want, it seems, is for her to do the job for which she is paid her commissions. Unfeeling brutes!

Dilly's basic problem is that she is no salesperson. She can *converse* with people, and sometimes she can even amuse them, but that's about it. So, soon bereft of clients, sales, and commissions, Dilly must painfully face reality, which she does by deciding that selling on commission is "unchallenging." Now her eyes turn to the corporate world. There, she reasons, she could be a *real* executive, getting paid a proper fixed salary for using her great talent, instead of merely having to "exploit people," which "runs counter to her nature."

Once again, Dilly is likely to meet with some initial success. She is intelligent, she is educated, she is technically well qualified, and she is "good with people," or so some of them say. Consequently, Dilly may well land a reasonably responsible staff role, most likely in advertising, public relations, or personnel. More to the point, however, is that Dilly is likely to be given an impressive-sounding title of some kind, a generous salary, her own office, and a secretary—perhaps even a male one. Oh, happy day for Dilly! All her great talents have finally been crowned with the success she has deserved so long. Or so it seems.

The problem is that actually having to *do* this fine job makes Dilly's head swim. She knows what she *ought* to be doing, but, for reasons that are unaccountable to her, she does "silly things" instead. Though her taste in clothes, guided by designer labels, remains excellent, her business judgment proves to be just awful. Indeed, despite her intelligence and her degrees, she often seems utterly witless. Her superiors, unable to figure out why, send her on intensive training courses, where quite often she shines: she is, after all, great in role-playing situations because she has been acting all her life. Having strong needs for structure, she is a quick learner when offered prepackaged solutions to problems, in this case business management problems.

Back on the job, however, the pressure returns, and once again real-life situations don't seem quite as simple. And now Dilly becomes frightened, and gets herself into a *real* pickle. At first, she tries to go by the book all the time, or, whenever she can't do that, tries to push the problem to another department. When both fail, she procrastinates—dillies and dallies—all the while trying to maintain her bright and bubbly facade. The whole act, however, is just a little too shrill, and now the big boss himself is beginning to have very serious doubts about Ms. Dilly.

Things are not too hot on the home front, either. Dilly has probably married a nice but fairly ineffectual sort of fellow, whose lack of ambition she more and more comes to despise.

He, poor devil, even if somewhat weak, is quite likely reasonably well adjusted, and thus does take his own job pretty seriously. He goes on providing for Dilly and the kids as best he can, while Dilly increasingly looks down upon his commitment as further proof of his menial mind-set. She thinks he should somehow do much better for himself, and for them both. What Dilly has failed to appreciate, and will continue to prefer to avoid knowing, is that, however weak her husband may or may not be, he is far, far stronger than she, because, whatever his faults, he goes on bringing home the bacon. It may not look like a big slice of bacon to Dilly, but it is invariably more than she imagines, and always more than she herself could make over the long haul.

What happens to Dillys in the end? Usually, if they don't quit first, they somehow get squeezed out or flat fired. In large American corporations, however, under current laws, it is often impossible to choke out all the Dillys, the result being that they are squeezed into highly structured roles where they can do no real harm while doing everything by the book. To make things "look right," frequently they get to keep the office, the title, the secretary, and often even all of the money.

Such a role might seem to be Dilly's American dream come true, but she will never live happily ever after because in her heart she will know that this is not the success whereof she dreamed, and thus will continue to feel as impotent as ever. She may even sense that she is on the way to becoming an office joke.

For a while Dilly will continue to find ways of winning attention, often by doing things that seem incredibly senseless to those about her. It is likely that she will also pester her boss to allow her to sit in with the real movers and shakers. When it finally becomes clear that the boss is never going to respond,

Dilly's schoolgirl manner will begin to reflect her unhappy despair. She will fume at her dilemma, pout at her boss, and pour spleen upon her husband, until she becomes eligible for early retirement, at which point she will be quietly eased out.

DILLY IN BRIEF

BASIC TYPE:	Dilettante, a breathless amateur.
ROLE-MODELS/HEROES:	Nancy Reagan, first lady of the United States. Corazón Aquino, president of the Philippines. Geraldine Ferraro, former candidate for vice-president of the United States. Jane Pfeiffer, former vice-president of NBC.
FACADE:	Effervescent, apparently confident, "presents well."
COFFEE TABLE LITERATURE:	*My Story,* by Geraldine Ferraro. *Working Woman* magazine.
FAVORITE SAYINGS:	"I want a job in keeping with my talent." "Oops! I seem to have made a little boo-boo." "Oh, dear! Something seems to have gone wrong, *again!*"
APPARENT OBJECTIVE:	To become a serious corporate gameplayer.
REAL OBJECTIVE:	To gain attention, status, and praise.

UNDERLYING EMOTIONS:	Unhappy, anxious, ambivalent towards most people including boss and husband.
BEDSIDE READING:	*True Romance.* Mail order catalogue for *Alcott & Andrews* female business attire.
MIGHT BENEFIT FROM READING:	*Good Housekeeping* magazine.
MANAGEMENT STYLE:	Autocratic bumbler.
STRENGTHS:	Intelligent, educated, attractive.
WEAKNESSES:	Lacks dedication or perseverance. Disintegrates when called upon to perform.
HOW TO SPOT:	Re-entering work force. Independent means, by way of spouse or possibly inherited money. Prior job instability. Refers to her "talent." Prior sales experience. A little too "personable." Seeks "people contact," visibility. Designer-label clothes.

Seeks "much more than" secretarial role.

HOW TO MANAGE: Avoid hiring, if possible. If not, structure role closely, and pay very modestly.

20

Holding the team together...

McCOY

Management is not being brilliant. Management is being conscientious. Beware the genius manager. Management is doing a very few simple things and doing them well. You put brilliant people into staff roles, but for Chrissake don't let them ever make decisions, because the secret of management is never to make a decision which ordinary human beings can't carry out. . . .
Management is craftsmanship.
PETER F. DRUCKER

McCOY is an authentic executive, a genuine person, an outstanding performer. He may or may not be a Scot, but, wherever in the world he's from, you can be sure that he's the *real* McCoy.

What's so special about him? On the surface, not too much. McCoy is no superman: not seven feet tall, seldom possessed of a fruity or stentorian voice, unlikely to be a snappy dresser. Some people might even call McCoy a somewhat ordinary guy. That is to badly underestimate him, however.

Before we get into just what it is that makes McCoy so great, let's first look at the eleven key qualities that are built solidly into such people.

Energy. McCoy is gifted with a great constitution. He's

strong, moves quickly, seldom gets tired, and bounces right back from virtually any difficulty or problem. He rarely gets sick, and when he does, it's never for long. There's something of a spring in his step, he likes to be on the go, and he's always doing something. When he's not at work, he's out playing, either with his kids, or golf or tennis with his wife, or down at the squash club with a few of the fellows. Friends may call him a "workaholic." Actually, he's a "livaholic."

Industry. The work ethic was instilled in McCoy when he was a boy. He came from a family of hard workers, and he grew up expecting to have to make a solid effort to get whatever he wanted out of life. He ran a paper route as a kid, and worked to help pay his way through college. He probably paid board to his parents, too. Now, as a man, McCoy finds that he is unhappy unless he's engaged in some kind of constructive activity. So work is never a chore to him, but an outlet for that energy he very much enjoys.

Perseverance. McCoy never quits. He completes virtually every task to which he ever turns his attention. He never drops out of anything. He might not have been the brightest kid in the class, but he still managed to complete all of his studies in the minimum time. He tends to regard obstacles as challenges, and he just keeps on trying to surmount them all the time. He likes to say that if enough people beat their heads against a brick wall, then the wall will fall down.

Self-reliance. McCoy's parents never pampered him. Instead, they taught him to stand on his own feet and learn from his mistakes. They encouraged him without making the mistake of giving him something for nothing. When he wanted money, they made him earn it. McCoy thus learned to depend upon himself to get the things he wanted or needed. Now, it's an instinctive, unquestioned reaction. When action is necessary, McCoy seldom looks around for help. Instead, he just goes out and does what has to be done.

Compatibility. Though not what you'd call a charmer, McCoy has a sound ability to get along with other people. He's not sarcastic, hostile, or abrasive. He treats everyone with more or less equal respect. He gets along about the same with superiors, peers, and subordinates and he also recognizes the importance of doing just that in achieving his own goals. McCoy is well liked off the job, too. People are happy to know him and he keeps long-term friendships.

Loyalty. A gentleman is a person who never uses the word, and the same is true of loyalty. McCoy never talks about being loyal, he just is. He rarely criticizes past employers, friends, or family. He's almost always willing to put the interests of others before his own. He identifies with his colleagues, and is happy to be on the team. He is essentially unselfish.

Leadership. People like to be around McCoy. He has the gift of making everyone else feel part of the team. He just naturally involves people in his and their overall goals. He can make mundane tasks seem very important. He also inspires confidence, admiration, and trust in others, so that people instinctively turn to him for help. Looking back over McCoy's life, you inevitably find that he has enjoyed quite a few positions of trust and leadership. And yet McCoy never gives one the feeling that he's *trying* to be a leader, or playing at the role. He just comes off as a very decent and regular guy trying to do something worthwhile, and who looks as if he will almost always succeed.

Motivation. One of the most important things about Mc-Coy is his motivation. He works because he derives a deep and often unconscious satisfaction from the task itself, the thing that he does. A close look normally reveals that his occupation fulfills a vital part of his early psychic scripting. He somehow came to believe that the only career worth having was in business management, thus he wants to be an executive the way some people want to be film stars. And he doesn't just want to *be* an executive, either, he also wants to *achieve* as an executive, for that way lie the rewards, both psychic and financial, that he uses as a measurement of his success and quality of life.

This kind of motivation comes from McCoy's parents, his role models, and the influence of the culture in which he was raised. McCoy's father was often a successful executive or businessperson, so McCoy is likely to be possessed of a strong unconscious drive to emulate him.

The influence of the culture is vital, too. In the United States, the successful businessman traditionally has been held to be a hero, so that the very best minds want to play the business game, and give of their very best at it. The English, on the other hand, continue to display a patronizing attitude to business: "A first-class pursuit for second-class minds" was the way an aristocratic friend of mine put it (little wonder that the expression "English executive" is something of an oxymoron). The point, anyway, is that McCoy is most likely to blossom in a suitable cultural climate.

Common sense. They say that if you've got common sense, you've got all the sense there is. Well, that's the kind of sense McCoy has. Although maybe not the brightest guy you ever met, McCoy seldom makes the same mistake twice, and he rarely—very rarely—makes stupid goofs, thus he never seems to get into serious trouble. He will never be taken in by get-rich-quick schemes, and he realizes that it's very smart to look out for the other guy's interests equally with his own. His private life adds up, too: he doesn't feel the need to date starlets, and his choice of a spouse reflects sound judgment. He can be romantic, but he's not starry-eyed. He can move very quickly when he has to, but he normally prefers to weigh his options about anything important. All in all, people agree that, no matter what the situation, McCoy will be quick to sum it up, and that he'll reach a pretty sound judgment.

Maturity. What this all really means is that McCoy has fully outgrown his childhood, and now demonstrates all the qualities of a true adult. He's not prone to childish wishful thinking, he's not thin-skinned or easily upset, he doesn't break down and cry or get angry under pressure, he's not given to petty jealousies, and he's free of self-destructive tendencies.

He has a few little quirks of his own, of course. He can become irked, and he can get down, and he has problems at home from time to time, as any spouse or parent normally does. McCoy never dwells on these things, however, and he never tries to make his problems anyone else's. He just deals with them as best he can as fast as he can, then moves on.

If McCoy does have a problem, it is likely to be that he's an obsessive-compulsive. Since he greatly enjoys what he does, he derives pleasure from working very hard at it, thus doesn't always want to go home when the hands on the clock hit five . . . or six . . . or seven. . . . McCoy's motto might be summed up in four words: "Without haste, but without rest." His wife would definitely say he's a workaholic. Working doesn't totally consume him, however, so that at least from his employer's point of view, his powerful commitment to it is a great blessing. All the same, it's something McCoy knows he has to be on guard against.

Stability. McCoy is not a job-hopper, but a long-term employee who stays around for two reasons. First, having made a sound choice of employer, he is happy to become part of a strong team that is trying to do something he sees as extremely worthwhile. Second, realizing just how valuable McCoy actually is to the enterprise, McCoy's employer makes every effort to keep him happy. McCoy gets promotions, and raises, and just quietly and gradually moves to the upper levels of management with a minimum of fuss, so there's no particular reason for him to want to relocate.

McCoy is usually stable in his private life, too. He normally marries only once, holds onto his friends, and keeps roughly the same recreational and leisure interests. He prefers to live in an area he has come to know well and grown comfortable with, thus thinks long and hard before selling his home. If he had to, he would relocate for the company, of course, or to get ahead if a really great opportunity came his way. Beyond that, he likes the sense of security of stable, well-known surroundings.

Is McCoy Boring?

McCoy can seem boring to people who imagine that an executive should look and act like the Hollywood stereotype of the genre, full of derring-do, rushing hither and yon, making an endless fuss, sorting out disasters, and taking incredible risks. McCoy is just not like that at all. His style is to get on and get things done in such a way that he never seems to be in trouble. McCoy is like a champion golfer who makes it all look easy by playing a percentage game, not trying to drive every green, or hole every approach shot when he misses, but simply staying in the middle of the fairway. He has some hidden reserves, of course, but he rarely seems to have to call upon them. But isn't he just a teeny bit boring? The answer is not at all.

Might McCoy Be Female?

Yes, of course McCoy can be female. However, the *chances* of McCoy being female are not so high as one might hope. The reason—as any psychologist would tell you—has to do with conditioning. To put it in a nutshell, males are conditioned to emulate their fathers, and thus the typical male's self-image is entirely tied up with becoming a "success" on the job, thereby earning enough money to support a traditional family in some kind of style. The drive to do these things isn't usually something he can even contemplate on a conscious level, because no other course seems open to him. His whole being is tied up with supporting his family, living up to parental and cultural expectations, and outperforming his father. And if he fails to do these things, *he judges himself to be a failure.*

The typical female, however, is much more fortunate, for she is not bound to such a script. Thus, while to be fired from a job is a blow to anyone, such an event is likely to be far more crushing to the male than to the female ego (though many males will furiously deny this fact). A woman in such circumstances is far more likely to be genuinely sanguine, to say that things didn't work out *in this instance,* and simply look around for something else to do, maybe in an entirely different field. She could sell the family house, and the car, and all the status symbols, and go and live in the woods, if need be, and still not feel any less of a person. Very few men, and certainly never a

McCoy, would be able to do that. A McCoy—male or female—gives the precious, palpable pulp of his or her being to the job and the role, for *that* is his or her mission and purpose in life. The way to find such a woman is simply to look at her past, and especially at her parents, her role models, her values, and her unconscious goals.

How Many McCoys Are There?

The McCoys of this world are infinitely fewer in number than most people will ever realize or accept. Genuine common sense is an uncommon quality to begin with, and then, in Western culture today, most people are just not psychologically well adjusted at all. North America, in particular, is home to a vast number of emotional pygmies who never become completely adult people.

So, if you run across a McCoy looking for employment, just grab him or her with both hands, then hang on with all your might.

MCCOY IN BRIEF

BASIC TYPE:	A genuine executive.
ROLE MODELS/HEROES:	Businessman father. Lee Iacocca.
FACADE:	Reasonable, calm, pleasant, keen to do a good job.
COFFEE TABLE LITERATURE:	*Wall Street Journal.* *Business Week.*
FAVORITE SAYINGS:	"That would be no problem." "Let's stick with it."
APPARENT OBJECTIVE:	To become a first-class executive.
REAL OBJECTIVE:	To emulate executive role model.
UNDERLYING EMOTIONS:	Keen to do the right thing, happy to be on the team, driven to give of his best.
BEDSIDE READING:	*Forbes.* *The Gamesman,* by Michael Maccoby.
MIGHT BENEFIT FROM READING:	*Wareham's Basic Business Types,* by John Wareham.
MANAGEMENT STYLE:	Calm, organized, confident, democratic.

STRENGTHS: Common sense, industry, people skills.

WEAKNESSES: None of major import.

HOW TO SPOT: Middle-class parents.
Businessman father.
Executive role models.
Graduated college in minimum time.
Earned business degree.
Ran small business to pay way through college, or maybe worked in family business.
Shows highly stable work history.
Appropriate demeanor and dress.
Probably has a sport or other interest that he takes seriously.
Lives within means.

HOW TO MANAGE: Coddle and caress him.
Promote him, pay him well.
Make him take regular annual vacations.
Never let him go.

EPILOGUE

THE TAPDANCING EXECUTIVE was the first "type" I ever committed to paper. He first appeared in a few business journals, then, later, in my book *Secrets of a Corporate Headhunter* (Atheneum, 1980). Subsequently, practically every reader of *Secrets* whom I met remembered and quoted the chapter on Tapdancer, explaining that some acquaintance or other fitted the mold. I also received an entire file full of correspondence from people who said they knew a Tapdancer, including a letter from a former forger who wrote to me from prison saying he'd read my book in the prison library and had been amazed to discover himself peering back out of the pages, for, yes, *he* was Tapdancer personified. His reason for writing, he said, was to inquire as to whether I might be able to tell him how to stop being a Tapdancer.*

In view of all the interest in Tapdancer, I'm including him again. If you haven't read about Tapdancer before, I hope you like him (or her, I'm sure). Even if you have read of Tapdancer before, you might just like to look him/her over one more time, because, after all, you wouldn't want to hire such a person just because you couldn't remember the type.

*By way of reply I sent him a copy of my book *Wareham's Way: Escaping the Judas Trap*, which I hope was of some help.

Waiting in reception for a job interview, and looking good . . .

TAPDANCER

When you go to dance, take heed whom you hold by the hand.
PROVERB

A TAPDANCING EXECUTIVE is not really an executive at all.

He appears to be the very quintessence of effectiveness, earnestly hurrying from meeting to meeting and memo to memo. He looks like an executive, acts, talks, commutes, eats, breathes, and laughs like one. It is difficult—impossible, in fact, for a casual observer—to differentiate between Tapdancer and the television version of a tycoon; the very similarity between these two offers a clue to organization watchers, however, for, above all else, Tapdancer is a performer.

He is a song-and-dance man with the capacity to hold an audience. He is just not an executive, however, for, when you get beyond the impeccable puff and the pretty smile, he just never *produces*, he just never makes or helps to make a profit.

Notwithstanding this fact, some organizations almost systematically recruit Tapdancers to many middle-management positions. This is not because of any desire to build an organization of song-and-dance men, but simply because Tapdancer's personality masks his problems, and nowhere more so than in an employment interview.

Tapdancer's Personality

Tapdancer's personality is characterized by good-natured extroversion and by bland charm. Tapdancers are affable, friendly, bright, enthusiastic, surgent, and role-aware. They are at ease in an interview, having the capacity to relax and to talk fluently while saying very little. Engaging, likable individuals, they naturally involve the interviewer, and thereby lead him to suspend his objectivity.

Tapdancers are pleasantly ingratiating, and spontaneously flattering. They have the knack of moving effortlessly to first-name terms, and of making instant friendships. The extroversion is not an act, but springs from a desire to be liked and a deep-seated wish to please.

Tapdancer rarely displays hostility, even in situations where another reasonably placid executive might become irritated. Tapdancer acquits himself excellently at an interview, often doubly so, for he has had more experience of the interview situation than most interviewers, and knows his part by heart. He is also likely to have been in far tighter situations than an employment interview. Many interviewers mistake the bland manner for simple self-control. But, for Tapdancer, this is a facade, and behind the facade there is nothing.

Tapdancer's intelligence is seldom above average, and it is often quite low. Tapdancers do, however, possess a polish that is normally associated with an above-average intellect. People normally assume that Tapdancer is intelligent because he *seems* intelligent; they mistake extroversion and charm for verbal skills. A skilled interviewer notices that Tapdancer has difficulty in pursuing a discussion to a logical conclusion. Tapdancer usually steers his interrogator away from such a discussion, however, with a well-honed skill, for he knows that it is upon the dance and not the dancer that the spotlight must fall.

The well-known "halo" effect, whereby an interviewee is rated highly on all skills because the interviewer likes him, always operates in favor of Tapdancer. He knows that he has the knack of "handling interviews" and so his confidence is quite well founded.

Tapdancer is not always a conscious manipulator of people, for he often lacks the raw intelligence to set about logical deception. His skills are strongest at the secondary subconscious level. Indeed, if Tapdancer knew exactly how he achieved his results, then he might move into the realm of being an effective executive. But he does not. There is no center to his personality. You seek for the center, and the center is hollow. No core, no edge, no bite, no sting—just a bland charm and friendliness that are very easily mistaken for the assurance of a competent executive on top of his job.

Tapdancers are seldom uncovered by psychological-temperament questionnaires. They score well on sales tests, show little or no anxiety, and achieve above-average scores on other factors normally associated with executive success.

Tapdancer's Appearance

Tapdancers are well-dressed, socially aware people, quite fastidious about their appearance. Their clothes usually evidence a sound appreciation of trends and styles while not reflecting high fashion. They wear executive apparel and are usually well aware of particular totems and taboos. They may wear trenchcoats and carry attaché cases. Suits are pressed, and shirts smart. A particular flash of style may be noted, but this is never overdone. The whole effect normally inspires initial confidence in the heart of any interviewer. There is no malice to Tapdancer. He is concerned merely to please, and to be safely employed. Consequently he will impress as a good team person, someone well able to be part of an organization. Not a boat-rocker. Not a credit-grabber.

When actually employed, Tapdancer takes his tone from the corporate personality. If it is a shirt-sleeves organization, he will be a shirt-sleeves individual. This chameleon quality thus further marks Tapdancer as a highly desirable team player.

Tapdancer's Work Habits

Although Tapdancer seldom makes a valid contribution to profits, he never appears far from pulling off a spectacular "deal," or devising a wonderful marketing plan. He also has the capacity to dazzle superiors—especially superiors once or twice removed—with jargon and pleasant-sounding plans.

His desk displays symbols of his importance: a nameplate, notepaper headed "from the desk of," impressive trays of gold or silver, company emblems and the like. He normally works in the marketing, advertising, public relations, or personnel areas. He is attracted to quasi-professional organizations such as insurance broking, or big blue-chip companies. Employment within such an enterprise lends crucial credibility to Tapdancer, while also enabling him to disguise the fact that he is achieving nothing by writing memos, conducting interviews, "handling loose ends," or establishing "good public relations."

Most Tapdancers are drawn to what they call public relations for two reasons: they have the capacity to make idle time good fun, and it is impossible to quantify the results of their "work." Indeed, many Tapdancers are given high-visibility positions because of their appearance, demeanor, and wish for status. In such a role, Tapdancer may wine and dine clients, attend conventions, or "follow up on things." Never, however, do the fruits of his remarkable charm result in actual *sales,* for his wish to ingratiate himself with his listener is greater than any capacity actually to close a deal. This total lack of an effective cutting edge is central to the personality, and therefore to the work capacity, of Tapdancer.

When Tapdancer is not attending meetings, he loves to organize them, for this is often key to his survival. He talks, shines, agrees, goes along with the conventional wisdom, and all before a live audience. His command of jargon and buzzwords is usually greater than other participants', and it is almost impossible to detect his illogicality along with the red herrings raised at every meeting.

Tapdancer's lack of intellect or focus usually goes unnoticed in a meeting, which, to him, is just another interview, but with a bigger audience. Tapdancer is fond of "democratic participative" management styles. In the course of any conference, he can happily support and reconcile opposing views. He likes open free-ranging discussions of options, viable alternatives, and marketing strategies. He never suggests conclusions or positive action. In the end, of course, he will always come down on the side of the majority, or the chief executive, whichever predominates. It is, of course, impossible to spot Tapdancer in such an environment. Indeed, many will warm to Tapdancer's nonthreatening manner, and commend his sound common sense.

Tapdancer writes occasional lightweight articles for trade journals. Where such articles are published, his name and photograph are prominent, and copies are brought to the attention of management. Close examination of such articles normally reveals that absolutely nothing is being said, and that jargon is offered as wisdom. The point is that Tapdancers quite like to see their names in print, but lack the intellect to thread together any set of ideas along a common theme. It is not unusual for the published articles of Tapdancer to be a paraphrase of some other lightweight article, or even straight plagiarism.

Tapdancers are prone to absenteeism, irregular hours, and procrastination. In every case, this is a means of coping with the conflict inherent in the work situation. That conflict stems from the fact that Tapdancer cannot function as an effective executive: he simply lacks the cutting edge, the focus, and the intelligence. He handles this situation by dazzling his colleagues with charm, guile, jargon, and the promise of pie in the sky. It is an act that will finally always be exposed, but this will take time in a large organization. When pressed to show results, he becomes ill or absent for any number of reasons. He arrives late and leaves early, and spends even more time out of the office on public relations exercises.

A common ploy is to join a great number of professional and trade organizations and be elected to their committees. This, it will be advised, is "good PR" for his employer, who cannot then deny him time out of the office (or even in the office) to serve such worthy causes.

Similarly, Tapdancer will enroll in management programs for which the only entry qualification is the ability to pay a fee (which he may collect from his employer), and at the end of which he will receive a diploma to hang on his office wall or to display at future interviews.

Tapdancers are particularly fond of speech-making opportunities, as they provide an almost perfect means for self-advancement while winning applause. They are not outstanding speakers because they lack depth of feeling or any thread of logic, but they will, nonetheless, acquit themselves far better than the average stage-shy executive.

Tapdancer's Income and Life-style

Tapdancer is unlikely to seek—or be earning—a high income at the time of being interviewed. Once aboard, however, he may be given a raise in view of his imagined "potential." He might later even gull some kind of mentor into sponsoring his membership on the management team, thereby "justifying" a similar salary to his colleagues.

Tapdancer's typical life-style is well described as transient. He is rarely "settled" and his private life is characterized by an inability to maintain any sort of deep relationship. He may well be impotent off the job, too. It is likely that he has never married, or, if he has, that the marriage has broken up. Where a marriage is claimed or does in fact exist, the partner is usually a well-bred, socially desirable person not without substance in the way of family wealth. Tapdancer does not usually produce children, or if he does, seldom takes the responsibility seriously.

Tapdancer is normally in the process of changing residence, and frequently lives in rented premises, or with friends, or in a hotel. He will speak of buying a house; thus his colleagues may assume that he is a normal suburban commuter. Such is not usually the case.

Tapdancer may frequently be seen around airports, international hotels, and the more fashionable parts of town. His social awareness gives him an appreciation of these places and he enjoys their supposed glamour. He realizes that other people are impressed by his ease in dealing with the personnel of high-status clubs, bars, and restaurants, and his genuine ability to be at home in such surroundings. His comparatively low income does not permit him to spend heavily in these haunts, but he will order well if buying a client lunch.

Mobility is a keynote of Tapdancer, for, ultimately, his inability to perform will necessitate his leaving most employers. His search for a new job will very often entail travel to cities or even countries far from his home. There is a double value in his mobility, because he enjoys the travel and it provides an entirely new set of people for him to charm. He will use the very fact that he is from some glamorous far-off place to gain employment interviews with relatively unsuspecting employers. His transience and lack of apparent roots will be explained by the fact of his emigration.

One particularly charming Tapdancer completed documentation at three Wareham offices in two countries—and not one job on any set of forms was the same. A telephone reference check from a previous employer was quite favorable, describing him as "pleasant, easygoing, good team man with a ton of potential."

The point to note here is that Tapdancers have excellent survival skills, developed over many years. Tapdancer, as distinct from run-of-the-mill incompetents, is seldom fired. He moves before the fall of the axe and makes a polished departure that may include a pretty speech and a polite note; for this reason, it is difficult to establish his effectiveness with past employers.

How to Handle a Tapdancer

The way to handle Tapdancer is never to hire him in the first place, which is easier said than done, for he is plausible, empathetic, and possessed of an astonishing capacity to disarm most interviewers.

Tapdancers are often first-class liars, too, sometimes pathologically so. The lie seems to conjure no guilt at all, and when an interviewer points to an inconsistency, or even produces evidence of a lie, Tapdancer is able to explain away the "error" in a bland, plausible manner.

Because he feels at liberty to "massage" his life history, his résumé can never be taken at face value. In the final analysis, the only way to nail him to the wall is to insist upon a detailed month-by-month account of every job since leaving school. Then, typically, he will produce a defense to this approach by explaining that large chunks of his work history have been in distant lands and have become, with the passage of time, very difficult to verify.

Some companies, he will explain, have changed or merged or simply faded into oblivion. Addresses and contacts will be proffered, however, and written references—bogus or real— might even be available. In some cases, the contacts may exist, but usually they do not. Reality and fantasy merge and it becomes impossible to check all leads without investing an inordinate amount of time.

Recognition of the genre is the prime weapon of the interviewer, and it must begin with the ability to suspect executives who at first blush seem too good to be true.

TAPDANCER IN BRIEF

BASIC TYPE:	Counterfeit executive.
ROLE MODELS/HEROES:	Bert Lance, former head of the United States Office of Management and the Budget. Gary Hart, former candidate for president of the United States. Michael Deaver, former White House public relations counsel.
FACADE:	Warmhearted, affable, good fun, company man.
COFFEE-TABLE LITERATURE:	*Wall Street Journal.* *Business Week.* *Advertising Age.* *Forbes.*
FAVORITE SAYINGS:	"I'm pretty strong on interface." "Let's call a meeting and air tactics." "What we need is some strategizing."
APPARENT OBJECTIVE:	To contribute to the team.
REAL OBJECTIVE:	To survive in a corporate setting.
UNDERLYING EMOTIONS:	Passive, dependent, insecure, anxious.

BEDSIDE READING:	*How to Succeed in Business Without Really Trying,* by Sheperd Mead.
MIGHT BENEFIT FROM READING:	*Wareham's Way: Escaping the Judas Trap,* by John Wareham.
MANAGEMENT STYLE:	Fuzzy democratic-participative.
STRENGTHS:	Bright personality. Useful interpersonal skills.
WEAKNESSES:	Impotent. Not very intelligent. Not interested in hard work. Potential or actual sociopath. Out and out liar.
HOW TO SPOT:	Currently between jobs for apparently sound reason. Seeks job in advertising, public relations, personnel, or any staff role. Socially aware, charming, confident, pleasant. Salary expectations less than might be expected. City of birth far removed from place of work. Worked in several cities or countries. Cites work history in terms of years only.

"Cannot remember" details
of earlier employment.

No bona fide academic
qualifications.

Affiliation with—and
certificates from—
management
organizations and quasi-
academic bodies.

Claims multiple degrees or
doctorate.

Single, or "between
marriages."

Transient dwelling.

Acquits self well at
employment interview.

Seems eminently
employable.

HOW TO MANAGE: Shun.

John Wareham was born in New Zealand, where he attended Victoria University of Wellington, graduated with a degree in business administration, and qualified both as a chartered accountant and an economist.

He founded Wareham Associates, an executive search and appraisal firm, in 1964, and has since extended its operations onto three continents, with headquarters in New York.

Having devoted nearly half a lifetime to researching and appraising executive behavior, John Wareham has become a foremost authority upon the subject. Many of his methods have become touchstones of personnel practice. His *Secrets of a Corporate Headhunter* and *Wareham's Way* are widely regarded as indispensable and classic guides to the human side of management.